Black British Members of Parliament
in the House of Commons

Black British Members of Parliament in the House of Commons
22 Stories of Passion, Achievement and Success

Published by Envision Publishing, UK.
www.envisionpublishing.co.uk

© Shirley Anstis, 2020
Words and Concept by Shirley Anstis
ISBN 978-0-9569480-4-5

Designed and illustrated by Yaa Agyapong and Labiba Haque, students
in the Department of Typography & Graphic Communication, University
of Reading. See typography.network/real-jobs-scheme

BLACK BRITISH MEMBERS OF PARLIAMENT IN THE HOUSE OF COMMONS

22 STORIES OF PASSION, ACHIEVEMENT AND SUCCESS

Words and concept by Shirley Anstis
Foreword by Lord Simon Woolley

Envision Publishing

Courage is the most important of all virtues, because without courage you can't practice any other virtue consistently.

— Maya Angelou

CONTENTS

ACKNOWLEDGEMENTS

Thanks to Julia and Leena who read the manuscript and offered valuable advice. Thanks to Laurie for encouraging me towards completion and giving me the space to do so. Thanks to Helen Jones for her brilliant editing.

Thanks also to Bim Afolami MP and Helen Grant MP for responding to my questions. I am grateful to my Member of Parliament, Matt Rodda, for helping me to secure a quote from David Lammy MP. A special thank you to Lord Simon Woolley for writing such a passionate foreword. It's a pleasure to finally share this book with you.

FOREWORD

I love this book. It's simple, straight forward and yet at the same time fantastically complex. Above all, though it is wonderfully inspiring.

I know all of the 22 members of Parliament from African/Caribbean heritage, some extremely well, such as my dear friend Diane Abbott, the first Black British female MP to enter the House of Commons. A stronger, greater role model for young women, Black and white, Diane would be difficult to beat, not least because throughout most of her time she's had to fight racism externally, and internally from her own party.

I'm also particularly biased to those MPs who have come through Operation Black Vote's mentoring schemes such as the trailblazer Helen Grant, who became the first Black female Conservative Minister, Abena Oppong-Asare and shadow Ministers former and present; Clive Lewis and Marsha de Cordova. But all these MPs have wonderfully moving stories – many I know up-close – and equally important is that they come from both sides of the political divide.

For any parent wishing to tell their children our story, the stories in this book should not go a miss. But this should also start a conversation for all those included in this book too. Truth is we have something special in common. We might have different political persuasions, but sadly with the way the world negatively views us, whilst that must not define us, we must not ignore the systemic racial inequalities that still persist. If we are to inspire a generation to follow in our political footsteps and change our world, at a level that goes way beyond party politics, we must have greater unity amongst ourselves.

I look forward to the 2nd and 3rd editions, with many more joining the ranks and our collective voices saying, "this is our parliament, our voices and we will be listened to".

— Lord Simon Woolley

INTRODUCTION

It all started when I worked as a Careers Adviser with secondary and college-aged young people. On one occasion I was expected to support students through a college careers event around business. I distinctly remember one workshop where the tutor mentioned several UK and international businesses to motivate young people. One student asked about any companies owned by Black people and the tutor responded that they didn't exist. I saw the student's face drop and his attention escape the room. He had switched off.

Although this was troubling for me to see I wasn't able to support him in that moment. I pondered this for a while and knowing that it wasn't true, wondered what would have been a better approach. This was about 15 years ago and I hope a lot has changed since.

But what could the tutor have done to address the needs of all the students? He could have given examples of airline companies which exist all over the world. There are wealthy Black sportspeople and performers, each one a business in itself. There are Black Prime Ministers managing the wealth of their countries. He could have highlighted senior Black staff in global corporations and identified local businesses such as restaurants, corner shops, taxi companies, hair salons and barbershops. He could have tracked down Black accountants, lawyers, bankers and insurers working in the business sector.

But it never occurred to him that his session would not motivate and connect to all the students. From history we learn, that the African American Madam CJ Walker was the first self-made female millionaire. There is now a Netflix series on her story. This event also reinforced my belief in the impact of role models. It is said that we need to see ourselves reflected in different sectors to believe it is possible for us to do something similar.

During my teenage years I remember hearing a speech by the African American civil rights leader, the Reverend Jesse Jackson in which he used the quote "If your mind can conceive it, you can achieve it." Over the years I've found this quote sitting at the back of my mind, to be leaned on when necessary.

My childhood in the Caribbean provided me with role models in every sector – banking, education, agriculture, medicine, politics, faith, tourism, sport, law, journalism and entrepreneurship. The young people at the college that day couldn't see it and were told it didn't exist.

Many of the Members of Parliament in this book will be firsts in some way. They would have imagined it to be possible even though they hadn't seen it. A few of them are household names but many are not. I hope this collection brings these trailblazers to a wider audience and serves to normalise political participation. Politicians are as flawed and human as the rest of us and I think we can attract a broader range of people if we can be more generous and less critical of them as fellow human beings. As Black people, we can fully engage with the political process, from voting to party members to contending party leadership. No one can represent all our needs, and anyone can let us down, but we do well to encourage those who have the skills, a desire to serve and the opportunity to make a difference. My hope is to encourage participation and pride in young and old alike.

This book is not intended to be party political and tries to retell the views of the people included. As new Member of Parliament Bell Ribeiro-Addy states in her maiden speech, her route to Parliament and that of many Black MPs is not the well-known one of "power, privilege, connection or wealth" (HC Deb 30 January 2020). In each of their stories, you will see the passions, achievements and service that bring them success. Each story, each journey, is unique and personal.

THE UK PARLIAMENT

The UK Parliament is one of the oldest in the world. It is made up of two parts: The House of Commons and The House of Lords. There are 650 Members of Parliament in the House of Commons and about 800 members of the House of Lords. Together they make the laws that govern the country. The Prime Minister and his or her team of MPs, known as the Cabinet, lead the country. There are always debates between the government and the opposition parties.

Without Parliament, it would be hard to maintain a civilised and largely safe society. It is impossible for everyone to be consulted regularly so politicians often make decisions on our behalf. Often times they need to choose between the community they serve (constituents), their party and their own conscience. The choice can be a weighty one as it may mean they are promoted within their party, banished to the backbenches or they lose their seat completely. I think the job is a complex and challenging one. For some individuals, it can be the best fit for their skills, passions and what they would like to achieve.

In recent years political discourse has become emotive, polarising and self-serving. This is partly due to the destabilising effects of global conflicts, the increasing disparity between rich and poor, the increasing awareness of our human impact on the planet, the use of technology to spread untrue messages, a desire for simple answers to complex questions and an awareness of the earth's dwindling resources. This has had an impact on several recent elections in the UK, USA, Europe and other parts of the world.

A TINY BIT OF HISTORY

The story of the United Kingdom is interwoven with global politics. Since the beginning of time, people have travelled across the world for trade, wealth and safety; humans seek survival.

From colonial times residents of the United Kingdom have wielded power and authority across the globe. As British people took to leading the world through the trade of goods and the dehumanising trade in people, the histories of Africans and Britons have become entwined. During the transatlantic slave trade, Africans were captured and forcibly taken to the Americas to work as slaves. This lasted for 400 years and the impact continues today. Many African countries were reshaped and exploited by European and African leaders.

As explained by David Olusoga in his book *Black and British*, British history includes those countries linked to Britain during the time of the British Empire. In particular, this includes India, countries in Africa and the Caribbean. In David's book, we learn too of the Black Tudors and other Africans in the British Isles who were not slaves. Miranda Kaufmann in her book *Black Tudors* focuses on several Black Britons who lived in Tudor England.

For many of us, our family stories weave different cultures and countries together. The BBC programme *Who Do You Think You Are?* is always a brilliant reminder of how mixed our ancestry could be even though we appear different in our ethnicity.

In this book, I profile Black and mixed-race Members of Parliament. My approach here is to give attention to those people who are using their passions and gifts to serve diverse communities across the United Kingdom. These MPs serve their whole community just like any other MP.

More than likely they would have experienced some prejudice or discrimination in their lives, but they have navigated themselves to a position where they have been chosen to represent one of the many mixed communities in the United Kingdom. Like other MPs, they have made themselves visible to serve despite the intrusion on their potential freedoms and their personal lives. The more visible they are the more praise and criticism they experience.

Both David Lammy MP and Diane Abbott MP have experienced a significant amount of hate literature that is not just political but also racist and scary. They appear to be resilient and continue to represent their constituents, but I imagine they must sometimes feel quite frightened and weary.

As a counsellor, I imagine that the emotional challenge must be incredible. It is a huge thing to accept that you will always disappoint someone, and all of your failures and successes are done in public.

All MPs can be held to account as elections provide the opportunity to cast your vote for or against your local MP. You can always go onto the Parliamentary website to check out how a member of Parliament has voted in any debate. You can access the various written and spoken contributions they've made in the House of Commons. This is one way to follow your MPs activities yourself and not rely on the media interpretations to inform you. You can speak to them, email them, lobby them and, eventually, vote them in and out.

A LOOK AT PARLIAMENTARY REPRESENTATION OVER THE YEARS

Black people do not necessarily share a set of political interests. We are as similar and diverse as any other ethnic group. Like other populations, the patterns of our electoral behaviour is affected by gender, class, education and geography amongst others.

Although Parliament lacks diversity, there has been some increase in representation over the years. There are 650 constituencies in the UK, each represented by an MP. The December 2019 elections saw an increase in non-white members from 52 to 65, an increase in women from 211 to 220 and an increase in those members who are openly LBGTQ, from 47 to 50. The last figure represents 7% of MPs. According to the Office for National Statistics (ONS), those identifying as lesbian, gay or bisexual make up 4% of the population. The government provide ethnicity figures for Black African (1.8%), Caribbean (1.1%), Black other (0.5%) and Black mixed (1.1%) totalling 4.5%. The 22 MPs here make up 3% of MPs. Interestingly both Labour and the Liberal Democrats have 50+ percentage of women MPs., the same figure as is represented in the general population.

Black and Mixed-race (Black and White) MPs will be the focus of this book as it seeks to find role models for another generation and celebrate successes. Following the December 2019 elections, there are 22 MPs whose stories will be shared here. It is aimed at encouraging more young people to see a future in politics as a possibility and to show them that despite the challenges, diversity in representation can match the diversity in all our communities. Not surprisingly there are many 'firsts' included:

- Diane Abbott is the first Black woman to become an MP

- Adam Afriyie is the first Mixed (Black/White) male Conservative MP

- Dawn Butler – as Minister for Young Citizens and Youth Engagement, became the first Black woman to speak from the Despatch Box

- Helen Grant is the first Mixed (Black/White) female Conservative MP

- Kwasi Kwarteng is the first Black African Conservative MP

- Chi Onwurah is Newcastle's first Black/mixed Member of Parliament

- Darren Henry is the first Black Caribbean Conservative MP

- Abena Oppong-Asare and Bell Ribeiro-Addy are the first MPs of Ghanaian heritage

- Kim Johnson is the first Black MP in Liverpool

- Claudia Webbe is the first female MP for Leicester East

The table that follows lists Black and Mixed MPs and the year they were elected. Following deaths, deselection and election losses over the years there are now 22 MPs serving. Their stories will be highlighted in the remainder of this book. Dawn Butler MP was elected in 2005, lost her seat in 2010 and was re-elected in 2015. Others who have lost their seats have not yet been re-elected.

Black and Mixed MPs and the year they were first elected

Year first elected	Black/ Mixed	Total BAME at the time	MPs
1987	3	4	Diane Abbott Paul Boateng Bernie Grant
1992	0	6	
1997	1	9	Oona King
2000	2	2	David Lammy Sir Mark Hendrick
2001	0	12	
2005	2	15	Adam Afriyie Dawn Butler
2010	5	27	Helen Grant Sam Gyimah Kwasi Kwarteng Chi Onwurah Chuka Umunna
2015	3	41	James Cleverly Clive Lewis Kate Osamor
2017	5	52	Bim Afolami Kemi Badenoch Marsha de Cordova Fiona Onasanya Eleanor Smith
2018	1	53	Janet Daby
2019	7	65	Florence Eshalomi Darren Henry Kim Johnson Abena Oppong-Asare Taiwo Owatemi Bell Ribeiro-Addy Claudia Webbe

MEMBERS OF PARLIAMENT

DIANE
ABBOTT

DIANE ABBOTT

Constituency: Hackney North and Stoke Newington
Party: Labour
Years in office: 1987 to present
Ethnicity: Black British (Caribbean)

Diane Abbott is the first Black woman to become a Member of Parliament in the House of Commons.

Diane was born in 1953 in Paddington, London to Jamaican parents. Her mother was a nurse and her father a welder. She attended a grammar school – Harrow County School for Girls, where she was the only Black pupil at the time. She was one of a few Black students to get into Newnham College Cambridge where she completed a degree, and a Masters, in History. She was married to the architect David Thompson and they have an adult son, James Abbott Thompson.

After university, she worked as a civil servant in the Home Office (1976–78), a race relations officer (1978–80) for the National Council for Civil Liberties (now Liberty) and as a television researcher and reporter (1980–84). This would lead to her becoming a press officer for the Greater London Council and Head of Press and Public Relations at Lambeth Council. During this time, she was a member of the Labour Party and active on issues of civil liberties. At 29 (1982) she was elected to Westminister City Council and served there until 1986. She was elected to Parliament in 1987 at the age of 34. She describes herself as a socialist.

Being passionate about education and aware of the under-attainment for Black children, she set up London Schools and the Black Child (LSBC) initiative in the 1990s. LSBC organised full-day conferences bringing parents, teachers, children, academics and policymakers together to address the complex issues around the underachievement of Black children and young people. The many workshops were all about celebrating successes and encouraging improvements in the teaching and learning of Black schoolchildren. It also presented awards to many high-achieving Black students who scored top marks in GCSEs, A levels and university courses.

In 1992 she also set up the not-for-profit organisation 'Black Women Mean Business' with the aim of celebrating and encouraging Black businesswomen in the UK.

Diane has been re-elected at every election since 1987! Despite constant criticism, her majority seems to increase after every election.

Like many MPs, she takes her role to represent her constituents and to improve people's lives seriously.

In her maiden speech on 16 November 1987, during the second reading of an Immigration Bill, we get a preview of the more recent Windrush Scandal. Diane noticed the "increasing restriction placed on movement, related to…quasi-racial categories: new Commonwealth, old Commonwealth…" (HC Deb 16 November 1987). At the time she was also hearing from many of her constituents who were frightened and confused by a new requirement to register, given that they had lived and worked legally in the UK for many years. The required £60 registration fee per person raised over £6 million for the government. She goes on to note that immigrants are not seen in good faith as people seeking to work and create a better life but as a "kind of plague or contagion. No measure is too botched up, too legally illiterate or too racist to keep them out." On criminalising overstayers and getting the police involved she predicts: "We will see what damage that will cause to police–community relations" (HC Deb 16 November 1987). The fear, administrative complexities, expense, police removals and hidden agendas are prescient of the hostile environment and Windrush scandal we are still unravelling.

In the 1980s and 1990s, Diane and her colleagues introduced or expanded on government bills that sought to improve the lives of many. This included issues as diverse as more accurate food labelling and introducing workplace nurseries and well-women clinics. She was also a supporter of bringing in the National Minimum Wage which is now a legal requirement. In December 1992 she joined several others in helping to bring about the Bill that would make racial violence a specific criminal offence.

Diane has become known for her support of human rights and was jointly awarded a special Human Rights Award in 2008, presented by the organisations Liberty, Justice and the Law Society. In the same year, she won the Spectator Parliamentarian Speech of the Year award.

In a debate in 2016 to review the 0.7% of the UK's gross national income that goes to foreign aid, Diane suggested that the best step forward is not to cut aid but to make non-governmental organisations (NGOs) more accountable and transparent. She also included the fact that even though the continent of Africa receives around US$30 billion in aid it loses US$192 billion in "debt repayments, lost tax revenue, tax transfers, multinational profits and other financial flows" (HC Deb 13 June 2016). Things are not always as they first appear.

Diane has been on both the treasury and foreign affairs committees. She has also held opposition posts for the Labour Party. She was appointed Shadow Minister for Public Health by Ed Miliband (2010–2013). Under the leadership of Jeremy Corbyn, she was appointed Shadow Secretary of State for International Development (2015–2016). Several reshuffles later she was promoted to Shadow Health Secretary and later the first Black female Shadow Home Secretary (2016–2020).

For many years Diane, alongside former Conservative MP Michael Portillo, appeared on the weekly BBC late-night politics show with Andrew Neil. She gave this up when she stood for the Labour leadership in 2010. The battle was won by Ed Miliband. Even though she did not win, Diane demonstrated a lot of confidence and then put herself forward for the London Mayoral elections in 2016. Sadiq Khan MP won the race to be Mayor of London and remains so today.

Diane has received lots of criticism in the media, and social media has opened the doors to increased online abuse. Tom Peck in *The Independent* noted that Diane Abbott received almost half of all abusive tweets sent to female MPs before the (2017) election. In a debate on online abuse on 12 July 2017 Diane suggests that there is a relationship between online abuse and mainstream media commentary. Like many others, she is concerned "about the degradation of public discourse online" (HC Deb 12 June 2017). On 13 June 2017, Diane spoke to the Guardian newspaper about her Type 2 diabetes diagnosis and the challenges of keeping healthy during an intense election campaign. She won her seat in 2017, and again in December 2019 with a majority of 33,188 from an electorate of 92,462, 61% of whom voted.

In February 2020 Diane questioned the deportation flights of Windrush descendants to Jamaica. She pointed out that they may not have had access to the required paperwork and would have found it difficult to communicate with legal advisers from a detention centre where access to technology and paperwork would be severely restricted.

She continues to pressure the government to reveal the extent of the catastrophe that is the Windrush scandal and to find out what they are doing to rectify the issues that have led to people being destitute or unfairly deported. She also continues to challenge the government on their response to knife crime, accusing them of using ineffective tools such as the indiscriminate use of stop and search but avoiding the discussion around cuts in policing and youth provision.

As one crisis is replaced by another the work of an MP is never done. On 4 May Diane was one of six MPs asking the government to 'take immediate action to address the unequal health and economic effects of COVID-19 on Black and other minority ethnic people. She joined other MPs to ask the government to change the experience for more than one hundred thousand migrant families who have a legal right to remain in the UK but no recourse to public funds. Many are destitute as they have lost their jobs and are unable to claim any benefits. This is ongoing.

We often get an incorrect sense of what people are like from the media's packaging of them. Diane was the daughter of working-class immigrants who worked her way to study at Cambridge University. She was the first female Black Member of Parliament in the UK; she contributed to hundreds of discussions and added her name to many parliamentary bills, improving the lives of many. Even her unsuccessful leadership bid helped to raise her profile and the areas she wants to impact, such as crime, civil liberties, immigration, health, education and international issues. She acts with conviction and a sense of responsibility. History shows that she defied the Labour Party leadership on the Iraq War and on tuition fees, both of which have been criticised a lot. Her underlying passion seems to be a desire for education, health, safety and equality for all regardless of age, race, gender or class.

SIR MARK
HENDRICK

SIR MARK HENDRICK

Constituency: Preston
Party: Labour and Co-operative
Years in office: 2000 to present
Ethnicity: Mixed British (White British and Black African)

Mark is one of 26 Labour and Co-operative MPs in the House of Commons. In order to become a Labour/Co-op MP, you need to be nominated by both the Labour Party and the Co-operative party, for the same seat and to be selected by both. The lesser-known Co-operative party brings cooperative values to politics. They are committed to building a society where power and wealth are shared. Other ideas include public ownership of the services and utilities we all rely on, more co-operative housing and credit unions to replace extortionate payday lenders. Mark is one of three Labour/Co-op MPs included in this book.

Mark Hendrick was born in 1958 in Salford to English and Somali parents. His father worked in the timber industry. He attended Salford Grammar School and then Liverpool Polytechnic (now Liverpool John Moores University) where he completed a degree in Electrical and Electronic Engineering. He followed this with a Masters in Computer Science from the University of Manchester. He is also a Chartered Engineer with a teaching qualification.

In 1979 at the age of 21, he followed his academic success with training as an engineer with the Ministry of Defence, at the Royal Signals and Radar Establishment. A couple of years later he joined AEG in Germany as a student engineer. In 1982 he was appointed as a Higher Professional to the Science and Engineering Research Council and remained with them until 1988. In 1990 he worked as a lecturer in Digital Electronics at Stockport College.

His route into politics began when he became secretary to the Salford Co-operative Party (1984–1994). After that, he was elected as a Salford City councillor (1987–1995). He was also the chairman of the Eccles Constituency Labour Party (1990–1994). From 1994 to 1999 he was elected to the European Parliament, representing Central Lancashire. His entry to the House of Commons came in the Preston by-election of 2000 following the death of the sitting MP Audrey Wise. He has been re-elected at every election since.

Mark has sat on the Foreign Affairs Select Committee (2012–2017) and the International Trade Select Committee (2018). His political interests include European affairs, foreign affairs, international development, defence and economic affairs. He currently sits on the Internal Trade Committee.

Over the years he has held several roles working with cabinet members when Labour was in power. He served as a Parliamentary Private Secretary in several departments. The role of Parliamentary Private Secretary (PPS) is seen as the first step to becoming a Minister. Others may simply like working with a Minister, being next to power without being accountable for all the decisions. Others may not get the promotion to Minister even if that is what they had hoped for. He has been a PPS to the following:

- The Secretary of State for the Environment, Food and Rural Affairs (2003–2006)

- Foreign Secretary, Margaret Beckett (2006–2007)

- Lord High Chancellor of Great Britain and Secretary of State for Justice, Jack Straw (2007–2008)

- Ivan Lewis, Minister of State for Foreign and Commonwealth Affairs (2009–2010).

In these departments, Sir Mark shows that he has a passion for the environment, justice and foreign affairs. His membership of All-Party groups shows that he is keen to promote good relations between the UK and other countries such as Germany, Norway and Singapore. He is also keen to explore the economic, social and ethical implications of Artificial Intelligence. Plus, he joins several other MPs in raising awareness of the harm that can come from excessive gambling.

He has questioned the government on many wide-ranging issues including health and social care, police funding, military job losses and Anglo-Russian relations. In October 2018 he introduced a debate to discuss home insulation so that more people could afford to have well-insulated homes. Sir Mark has been in Parliament as long as David Lammy MP but fewer members of the public know of him. Each MP finds the different ways in which they can contribute to their constituents and the country during their time of service. Sir Mark appears to be a very active local MP advocating for his constituency whenever the opportunity arises.

He successfully campaigned for the public to have free access to the National Football Museum and this was achieved in 2002. He also campaigned for Preston to get City Status and this was awarded in the Queen's Golden Jubilee Awards in 2002. For this and his Parliamentary and political service, he was appointed a Knight Bachelor in the Queen's 2018 New Year's Honours list. He held his seat in the December 2019 elections with a majority of 12,146 from an electorate of 59,672 with a 56% turnout.

DAVID
LAMMY

DAVID LAMMY

Constituency: Tottenham
Party: Labour
Years in office: 2000 to present
Ethnicity: Black British (Caribbean)

David was born in North London to Guyanese parents in 1972. He and his four siblings were raised by their mother. David grew up in Tottenham which he now represents in Parliament. As an early achiever, he won an award for a choral scholarship at the age of 10. This enabled him to sing at Peterborough Cathedral whilst attending The Kings School in Peterborough. He attributes part of his decision to go into politics as a result of his experience at this school; it was both very pastoral and a place where he experienced racism at the hands of pupils and teachers.

David went on to study law at the School of Oriental and African Studies, University of London. He was called to the bar in England and Wales in 1994, practising as a barrister. He then became the first Black Briton to study a Masters in Law at Harvard Law School, graduating in 1997. He is married to Nicola Green, a portrait painter, and they have three children.

David's political career began in 2000 when he was elected to represent Labour on the London Assembly. Later that year he stood in a by-election following the death of Bernie Grant.

In 2004 David Lammy, supported by seven MPs, including the Prime Minister, presented a bill to make new provision for people who lack mental capacity and to establish the Court of Protection.

David is part of several groups in the House of Commons that are made up of members from all political parties. These groups, All-Party Parliamentary Groups, seek to raise awareness of particular interests and promote innovative solutions. He is a member of All-Party Parliamentary groups on Fatherhood, Faith & Society, British Jews and British Caribbean politics. As a father, he is particularly keen that government legislation is familiar with the modern family set-up and encourages active and responsible fatherhood.

His ability has been seen in Parliament as he held many ministerial positions when Labour was in power.

- 2002 – Parliamentary Under-Secretary, Department of Health. Overseeing the introduction of four-hour waiting times in Accident and Emergency.

- 2003 – Minister in the Department for Constitutional Affairs, Media and Sport

- 2005 – Minister for Culture, Department of Culture, Media and Sport

- 2007 – Parliamentary Under-Secretary of State in the Department of Innovation, Universities and Skills

- 2008 – Promoted to Minister of State; Appointed to the Privy Council

- 2009 – Minister for Higher Education, Department for Business, Innovation and Skills. Establishing the Skills Funding Agency and the National Apprentice Service.

David appears to be a principled politician motivated by fairness and justice. He nominated Diane Abbott in the leadership contest so that the field would be diverse, even though he supported another candidate, David Miliband. He turned down a post in the Shadow Cabinet in 2010 so he could freely speak out against government cuts. In 2014 he put himself forward for London Mayoral elections but came fourth to Sadiq Khan, Tessa Jowell and Diane Abbott.

David has consistently spoken out on issues that disproportionally affect Black people and those from disadvantaged backgrounds. In 2013 he challenged the government's stance of fixed-odds betting, launching a campaign to stop this practice. The result in 2018 was that the government agreed to lower the stakes so that a maximum bet is £2.00, no doubt saving many from losing money.

He tries to hold the government to account on the London riots of 2011, the growth of knife crime, the failures of the criminal justice system, the lack of student diversity at Oxford University, the Grenfell Tower disaster (2017) and the Windrush Scandal (2018). He lost a friend, a talented creative, in the Grenfell Tower so the tragedy was also personal. His continual challenge for Oxford and Cambridge universities to improve ethnic diversity has led to Oxford investing in more outreach and Cambridge introducing a foundation year.

In April 2016 David brought the motion for better diversity at the BBC, given the fact that it has a Royal Charter and plays a major role as a public broadcaster. Fast forward to 2020 and progress has been made, with the BBC creating new roles under Director of Creative Diversity, June Sarpong MBE. However, a recent editorial decision to broadcast the 'N' word – on two occasions – shows that there is still a lot of work to be done.

In 2016 David launched the Save Our Apprenticeships campaign forcing the government to do a U-turn on funding cuts for young people in deprived areas. He also opposed government plans to privatise the Land Registry and these plans were stopped, keeping the Land Registry in public hands.

2016 was an incredibly busy year for David Lammy when he was also asked by the then Prime Minister, David Cameron, to set up an independent review of the outcomes for Black and minority ethnic individuals in the Criminal Justice System. The Lammy Review published in 2017 had 35 recommendations for improving the Criminal Justice System. Very few of these have been implemented and David has shared his disappointment about this recently.

On 14th June 2018, David spoke on the Windrush 70th anniversary debate. He took space to remember the 492 West Indian immigrants who arrived at Tilbury docks on 21 June 1948 as well as the 524,000 Commonwealth born people who came to the UK up to 1971. He paid tribute to these mainly young people who responded to an invitation to come and help rebuild a Britain crippled by war.

They worked in the National Health Service and as transport workers, bus and train drivers, cleaners, cooks and wardens. He highlighted the cultural and positive contributions made by Windrush descendants and also the struggle for survival that is felt in many Caribbean communities due to injustices like the murder of Stephen Lawrence.

He also referenced the toll of 300 years of slavery on the Caribbean. He suggests that the freedom from slavery in 1834 meant that these islands no longer had slaves and slave owners but "rich planters and landless, low-wage labourers" who worked in unbearable conditions with few benefits" (HC Deb, 14 June 2018). He noted that 12 million people had been forced into slavery over those 300 years. Britain has never faced justice for the crime of slavery; no reparations have been paid to the descendants of slaves but the debts to slave owners were being paid off as recently as 2015.

He is very proud to be a Member of Parliament but would also like to encourage a more complete teaching of the country's history as is done in other countries such as Japan and Germany. This helps citizens to look at good and bad in history so that the mistakes of the past are not repeated. He calls for a hardship fund for Windrush victims. He wonders why 32 Windrush citizens who were unlawfully deported have been refused their right to return. In his own constituency, he has been supporting 27 people with Windrush cases.

In December 2019 David held his seat with a majority of 30,175 from an electorate of 75,740 with a 62% turnout.

On 30th June 2020, regarding the lack of action by the government in response to the Lammy Review (2017), David commented: "History is littered with examples of what happens if we abandon good faith. Without good faith, people get angry. Without good faith, people take to the streets. Without good faith, people give up hope" (HC Deb 30 June 2020).

He felt that whilst the situation that prompted the review had got worse, the recommendations were not being implemented. He went on to say: "When I completed the review, 41% of children in prison came from a black, Asian or minority ethnic background – and now the proportion is 51%. The proportion of all stop and searches on black people has increased by 69% over five years. The average custodial sentence for a black person is almost 10 years longer than that for a white person. To recognise the pain of these injustices, the Government need to go further than my review went, not cover up for the recommendations they ignored" (HC Deb 30 June 2020).

David has managed to use social media to engage with complicated issues like the perception of the "white saviour". This was triggered by the way a journalist posed with a Black child on a Comic Relief trip. There was anger and backlash, but it got Comic Relief to reflect on who it uses, and how it carries out its work. David is an ambassador for Action Aid, Trustee of the National Youth Theatre and president of the British and Foreign School Society.

David was the first MP to call for a referendum on any Brexit deal. This did not happen, but it gained momentum across the country. In January 2020 he ruled himself out of the Labour leadership elections feeling there might be someone else better placed to unite the party and be trusted by the country.

In February 2020 he tried to lobby the government to stop a deportation flight to Jamaica. He reminded the House of the 164 people from the Windrush generation who were wrongly detained and deported. Additionally, he shared that 5,000 people were not given access to public services such as education, healthcare and pensions – despite being entitled to this. He knows that the government is getting much of this wrong but wonders why the review of the lessons learned has not been made available and why the deportation flights have been resumed. Is it possible that there are children and British nationals on the flights?

Since then, inspector Wendy Williams has published her review (March 2020) which showed the catastrophic outcomes for many who got caught in the government's hostile environment, created when Theresa May MP was Home Secretary. The review found evidence of institutional racism in the design and enforcement of the immigration laws, destroying the lives of hard-working, law-abiding citizens. Many have lost jobs, homes and been left destitute. A 2020 BBC feature-length factual drama – Sitting in Limbo – tells the story of Anthony Bryan who was caught up in the hostile environment.

Some have been deported back to countries they left as children over 50 years ago. More than 8,000 have proved that they were living here legally. David set up a specialist Commonwealth Taskforce and helped to establish a compensation scheme. Although there is a fund of more than £200 million, only £62,198 has been paid out to 36 people. David listens to his constituents, knows their stories of suffering and does not want the government to bury the truth.

You can learn more about David in his own words. He has written two well-received books – *Out of the Ashes: Britain after the riots* (2011) and *Tribes: How Our Need to Belong Can Make or Break the Society* (2020).

ADAM
AFRIYIE

ADAM AFRIYIE

Constituency: Windsor
Party: Conservative
Years in office: 2005 to present
Ethnicity: Mixed Race British (Black African/White British)

Adam, born in 1965, is the son of a white British mother and a Black Ghanaian father who grew up on a council estate in Peckham, south London. He lives in Old Windsor with his wife and five children. He gained a BSc in Agricultural Economics from Imperial College, Kent. He made the most of his Gap Year by visiting Israel, Egypt, Cyprus, Greece, Holland, Denmark and Sweden. Adam was the captain of his university basketball team and has remained a keen sportsman.

He has been the Parliamentary representative for Windsor since 2005. He entered politics after a very successful career in business, having founded several companies. Unlike most MPs, he has never claimed personal expenses for his role. I found several articles on Adam Afriyie by the mainstream press highlighting his wealth or whether he is the UK's Barack Obama.

He is passionate about business and enterprise, trade, social mobility, mental health, a simpler tax system plus science and innovation. As well as sitting on various committees he has been chair of the Parliamentary Office of Science and Technology. Most significantly he has been the Shadow Minister (Science and Innovation) from 2007 to 2010. He was appointed as the Prime Minister's Trade Envoy to Ghana (2016) and Guinea (2017). He continues to campaign against a third runway at Heathrow. He is a big believer in entrepreneurship as a means of social mobility. He was a governor of The Museum of London and con-tinues to be a Patron of Berkshire Young Enterprise. Other concerns are around flooding, making good use of technology and improvements in the mental health system.

In July 2006 Adam contributed to a debate in the Department of Health around human reproductive technologies. He questioned the government's decision to retrospectively remove donor anonymity and suggests it will have a negative effect on the supply of donors.

In the December 2019 elections, Adam held his seat with a majority of 20,079 from an electorate of 75,038 with a 72% turnout.

Adam is chair of the All-Party Parliamentary Group on Financial Technology, providing a space for Parliamentarians to discuss the opportunities and challenges relating to the Financial Technology industry.

Adam is a vice-chair of the All-Party Parliamentary Group on Heathrow Expansion and Regional Connectivity. Adam is a patron of the Parliamentary Space Committee.

DAWN BUTLER

DAWN BUTLER

Constituency: Brent South and Brent Central
Party: Labour
Years in office: 2005–2010 (Brent South) 2015 to present (Brent Central)
Ethnicity: Black British (Caribbean)

Dawn was born in London in 1969 to Jamaican parents. She went
to Tom Hood School in East London and Waltham Forest College.
Her foray into politics began when she became an officer
of the GMB Union. She would go on to be an adviser to former Mayor
of London, Ken Livingstone.

She first became a Labour Member of Parliament in 2005. She represented Brent South in London from 2005 to 2010. She was Minister
for Young Citizens and Youth Engagement from 2009 to 2010 under
Prime Minister Gordon Brown.

At the 2009 Women in Public Life Awards, Dawn was named female
MP of the year. With her appointment as Minister for Young Citizens
and Youth Engagement, she became the first Black woman to speak from
the Despatch Box.

Dawn lost her seat at the 2010 elections. During this time there
were changes to constituency boundaries. Despite the setback,
she was selected for the seat in 2015 and won it back. Not many MPs have
been re-elected after losing their seat.

Since 2016 she has served as Shadow Minister for Diverse
Communities. This changed in August 2017 when she was appointed
Shadow Secretary of State for Women and Equalities.

On 21 March 2017, United Nations International Day for the Elimination
of Racial Discrimination, Dawn spoke on the subject in the Commons.
She shared her concern for the surge in intolerance and lack of understanding of different communities. She went on to say "we should
be embracing differences; they make us stronger, not weaker. We should
be fighting poverty and global warming, not other human beings"
(HC Deb 21 March 2017).

At the 2019 Labour Party Conference she introduced Labour's plans
to make medium to large firms offer flexible working to women going
through the menopause. This shows that the work of MPs is never
complete and responds to what is expected in the culture. Maternal
leave, paternal leave and menopausal adjustments are what we expect

of modern working practices. She is also passionate about young people and is an honorary vice president of the British Youth Council.

In the December 2019 elections, Dawn held her seat with a majority of 20,870 from an electorate of 84,032 with a 58% turnout.

Dawn Butler is one of 15 MPs on the Caribbean All-Party Parliamentary Group. Dawn is a vice-chair of the All-Party Parliamentary Group on Music, connecting Parliament to the music industry. Dawn is a member of the Sickle Cell and Thalassaemia All-Party Parliamentary Group, seeking to reduce inequalities and improve standards of care.

Dawn is the chair of the All-Party Parliamentary Group for Governance and Inclusive Leadership. It seeks to raise the issue of inclusive leadership in all areas of society and tackle the barriers that prohibit some people from achieving positions of influence.

HELEN
GRANT

HELEN GRANT

Constituency: Maidstone and The Weald
Party: Conservative
Years in office: 2010 to present
Ethnicity: Mixed Race British (Black African and White British)

Helen's mother was white British and her father, an orthopaedic surgeon, was Black Nigerian. After her parents separated, she was raised in Carlisle on a council estate with three generations on her maternal side. She was born in 1961.

As a recipient of some racist bullying in her youth, she channelled that into sporting excellence. She represented Cumbria in athletics, tennis, cross-country and hockey. She was also an under-16 judo champion. Helen is married to Simon and they have two sons, one of whom has served in the Royal Marines.

Helen cites success in sport at school plus the never-ending support and encouragement from her mother and grandmother as the explanation for her being able to aim high.

She undertook a law degree at the University of Hull and, looking back, recognises the value of being able to get a grant at that time. After some political input, she attended the College of Law in Guildford. With some experience under her belt she set up her own firm, Grant's Solicitors, in 1996 specialising in family law. Interestingly, Grant joined the Labour Party in 2004 but became disappointed by them before joining the Conservatives in 2006.

One of her early memories is attending a women's refuge where her mother volunteered. This experience helped to lead her towards a career in family law. In corresponding with me Helen shared that she got into politics to "stretch myself, learn more and try to make a difference whilst building upon my previous career as a legal aid solicitor". Helen had a 23-year career in law and sees this as good preparation for the role of a constituency MP and the associated parliamentary work. She is keen to help individuals get a good outcome from difficult challenges, even if that means enduring all the shouting and heckling at Prime Ministers Questions.

Helen became a Conservative MP in 2010, becoming the first Mixed Black female to do so. She has served on several committees including international development and justice, business, foreign and commonwealth affairs as well as law and order, women, children and families.

In April 2016 Helen supported David Lammy in bringing a motion to discuss increasing diversity in the BBC, a public-funded broadcasting service. She was very clear to point out that this needs to be a sustainable change where skilled people can be recruited and promoted, representing the world we live in. Not tokenism.

In the December 2019 elections, Helen held her seat with a majority of 21,772 from an electorate of 76,109 with a 68% turnout.

Helen is a member of the Sickle Cell and Thalassaemia All-Party Parliamentary Group, seeking to reduce inequalities and improve standards of care. Helen is co-chair of the All-Party Parliamentary Group on Wine and Spirits, promoting the economic and commercial benefits of the UK wine and spirit trade to the UK economy.

**KWASI
KWARTENG**

KWASI KWARTENG

Constituency: Spelthorne
Party: Conservative
Years in office: 2010 to present
Ethnicity: Black British (Black African)

Kwasi was born in London in 1975 following his parents' relocation from Ghana in the 1960s. His father is an economist and his mother a barrister. Kwasi went to Eton College and won their prestigious Newcastle Scholarship prize before going to read classics and British history at Trinity College, Cambridge. He would go on to complete a PhD in the subject. He was on the Cambridge University team that won the BBC's University Challenge in 1995!

This led to him becoming a financial analyst in the city for seven years and later he worked as a journalist. As an author he has written several books; his first was *Ghosts of Empire* (2011), a look at the global legacy of the British Empire, published by Bloomsbury. He has since published several books covering Conservative thought, British Empire, money and Margaret Thatcher. He is passionate about conservativism, reducing the role of the state and increasing the impact of business enterprises.

In 2005–2006 he was chairman of the Bow Group – the UKs "oldest conservative think tank" (The Bow Group, 2020). Kwame was a Conservative candidate for Brent East at the 2005 General Election. He was also a candidate for the London Assembly in 2008. He was unsuccessful in both.

In 2010 Kwame was selected as the Conservative candidate for Spelthorne and he continues to represent that constituency. He became the first Black African Conservative MP. He has been a strong supporter of Brexit and campaigned to bring it into reality.

He became Parliamentary Private Secretary to the then Chancellor of the Exchequer Phillip Hammond in 2017. In 2018 he was a Minister in the Department for Exiting the EU.

In July 2019 he became a Minister of State at the Department for Business, Energy and Industrial Strategy as well as being appointed to the very elite Privy Council. He has also been a Parliamentary Private Secretary (PPS) to the Leader of the House of Lords.

In October 2019, as Minister for Business, Energy and Clean Growth Kwasi was working towards growing the number of hydro projects and encouraging the planting of UK-grown trees. Many issues around renewable energy, electrical vehicles and lowering carbon emissions fall in his department.

In the December 2019 elections, Kwasi held on to his seat with a majority of 18,393 from an electorate of 70,929 and a 70% turnout.

CHI
ONWURAH

CHI ONWURAH

Constituency: Newcastle upon Tyne Central
Party: Labour
Years in office: 2010 to present
Ethnicity: Mixed Race (Black African/White British)

Chi represents the constituency where she grew up.
She is Newcastle's first Black/mixed Member of Parliament. Her father, a Nigerian dental student, attended Newcastle University Medical School where he met and married her mother. She was born in Northumberland in 1965. Her mother's father was a sheet metal worker in the Tyneside shipyards in the 1930s, so the family were local to the area.

The family moved to Nigeria when she was a baby but the Biafran War there would see her mother return to Newcastle leaving her father to join the Biafran army. On her own website, she credits this experience as giving her a great appreciation for democracy where change can come about through the ballot box without the need to fight.

Chi has demonstrated skills and knowledge in many different fields. She graduated from Imperial College London with a BSc in Electrical Engineering. As a woman in technology in the 1980s, she would have been in a significant minority. She worked across hardware and software in the UK, Nigeria, France, Denmark and the United States.

She was an active member of the Anti-Apartheid Movement, a British organisation opposed to South Africa's Apartheid System that oppressed and persecuted non-whites. She was on its National Executive and served also on its successor organisation, ACTSA. As an MP she has an opportunity to use her skills in a more impactful way.

Chi studied for an MBA at Manchester Business School whilst working as an Engineer and gaining her Chartered Engineering status! She has also been on the Advisory Board of the Open University Business School because of her belief in educational opportunities for every age and at all levels. Immediately prior to becoming an MP, she was Head of Telecoms Technology for Ofcom, the UK Communications Regulator.

Since becoming an MP in 2010 she has had several positions. The first was as a Junior Shadow Minister for Business, Innovation and Skills, 2010. In 2013 she became a Shadow Minister in the Cabinet Office. In 2015 she was made a Shadow Minister for Business, Innovation and Skills as well as a Shadow Minister for Culture, Media and Sport. She's been the Shadow Minister for Industrial Strategy, Science and Innovation from October 2016 to the present day.

As she had been used to such low female representation in engineering the low numbers in Parliament did not put her off. She has been supportive of initiatives to improve the lives of women. She gave her support to the campaign Let Toys Be Toys (2014) highlighting the negative impact of gender stereotypes when very different toys are made for boys and girls. For her, it is not just a theoretical argument but one of the reasons for the falling percentage of women in courses (and subsequent professions) like engineering. For her, this is also an economic issue as engineering jobs pay well and contribute to the economy.

In 2015 Chi nominated Jeremy Corbyn for leadership of the Labour Party to broaden the debate. In an article in *The New Statesman*, she shared how, in the final analysis, Andy Burnham, was the candidate she wanted to win and would vote for.

She has a place in *Computer Weekly*'s Hall of Fame for Most Influential Women in UK IT in 2018 where she is described as "an advocate for digital skills and digital enablement" (McDonald, 2018).

On International Women's Day 2019 she held a Real Talk event inviting young women in Newcastle Central to come and speak to her about the issues that they were concerned about. In the December 2019 elections, she held her seat with a majority of 12,278 from an electorate of 57,845 with a 65% turnout.

Chi has been named one of the hardest working MPs and that is easy to understand when you see the many parliamentary groups she chairs or is a member of.

Chi is the chair of the following:

- All-Party Parliamentary Group on Angola which seeks a greater understanding of Angola in Parliament whilst supporting development and democracy.

- All-Party Parliamentary Group on Adult Education, celebrating its positive contribution to the UK and helping to raise its profile through changing policy.

- All-Party Parliamentary Group on Black, Asian and Minority Ethnic (BAME) Business Owners whose aim is to support the growth of successful BAME businesses for the benefit of the overall UK economy.

- All-Party Parliamentary Group for Creative Diversity.
  Its aim is to identify and tackle obstacles to diversity and inclusion

in the creative sector, establish effective practices and make recommendations to industry and government.

- All-Party Parliamentary Group on Diversity and Inclusion in Science, Technology, Engineering and Maths (STEM). The group seeks to encourage inclusion and progression of people from diverse backgrounds in STEM by working with Parliamentarians, businesses, academics and other stakeholders

She is also vice-chair of the following:

- All-Party Parliamentary Group for the Commonwealth. Its 16 members seek to strengthen the Commonwealth network whilst taking advantage of opportunities to network for Britain's political and commercial activities.

- All-Party Parliamentary Group on Internet, Communications and Technology which looks at the industry, related policies, consumer groups and other stakeholders.

- All-Party Parliamentary Group on Open Banking and Payments seeking to maintain competition, fairness, value, accessibility and innovation. She is a vice-chair of the All-Party Parliamentary Group on Personalised Medicine, promoters of innovative science in personalised healthcare such as genomics.

- All-Party Parliamentary Scientific committee which focuses on science and technology and provides a long-term link between Parliament, academia and industry.

- The Parliamentary Space Committee.

Chi sits on the All-Party Parliamentary Engineering Group. This keeps Parliamentarians involved with the world of engineering, especially the work of young engineers. She is also on the All-Party Parliamentary Group on Infrastructure, which highlights the importance of economic infrastructure in the UK to all stakeholders.

JAMES CLEVERLY

JAMES CLEVERLY

Constituency: Braintree
Party: Conservative
Years in office: 2015 to present
Ethnicity: Mixed race (Black African/White British)

James was born in Lewisham in 1969 and was privately educated
in Lee, both in South London. His father is white and a surveyor whilst
his mother is a midwife who came from Sierra Leone. He is married with
two children.

James spent some time in the army (1988–1989) before this
was cut short when he suffered a leg injury. His roles in the Royal Artillery
and Territorial Army went from second lieutenant (1991) to lieutenant
(1993) to captain (1998) and then major (2003). In 2015 he was promoted
to lieutenant colonel.

Outside of the army, he completed a bachelor's degree in Hospitality
Management from what is now the University of West London.
He followed this with various jobs in publishing, eventually becoming
Head of Digital Media for Caspian Publishing (2006) and becoming
the co-founder of Point and Fire, a web publishing company.

His political success did not come easily to him as he had been
unsuccessful in many previous attempts. He was not chosen in Lewisham
Borough Council elections (2002), Lewisham Borough council by-election
(2003), Lewisham East MP (2005) and Conservative candidate for Mayor
of Lewisham (2006).

James was elected as a Conservative assembly member for Bexley
and Bromley in 2008 and was a representative on various bodies such
as the Greater London Authority, London Development Agency board
and the Metropolitan Police Authority. His role was to support the Mayor
to reduce youth offending.

When Boris Johnson was Mayor of London, he appointed James
in the new role of Mayor of London's youth ambassador (2009). This
was soon followed by James becoming chairman of the London Waste
and Recycling Board (2010) and chair of the London Fire and Emergency
Planning Authority (2012). He was then nominated to represent
Bexley and Bromley in the 2012 Greater London Authority elections
and won the seat.

In 2015 he was selected as the Conservative candidate for Braintree
and won the seat in the May elections of that year.

He has been a Minister without Portfolio and a co-chair of the Conservative Party since July 2019. Prior to this, he was Parliamentary Under-Secretary (Department for Exiting the European Union) from April to July 2019. James has also been a member of various committees including the International Trade Committee. He was a supporter of Brexit in the 2016 EU membership referendum.

In the December 2019 elections, he held his seat with a majority of 24,673 from an electorate of 75,208 with a 67% turnout.

James is a vice-chair of the All-Party Parliamentary Group Showing Racism the Red Card which aims to combat racism by enabling role models, especially footballers, to present anti-racism education to young people and others.

In July 2020 James was the Minister for the Middle East and North Africa. In September 2020 James is a Minister of State in the Foreign, Commonwealth and Development Office. These many positions over just a few years show that Ministers are expected to gain a wealth of knowledge to lead in a range of government departments.

CLIVE
LEWIS

CLIVE LEWIS

Constituency: Norwich South
Party: Labour
Years in office: 2015 to present
Ethnicity: Mixed race (Black Caribbean/White British)

Clive was born in London in 1971. He was raised by his father on a council estate in Northampton. His mother was English, and his father had emigrated from Grenada. He was the first member of his family to attend university.

Following his Economic degree at the University of Bradford, he was elected student union president, a first taste of political life. He later became vice president of the National Union of Students. In 1996 Lewis ran for president of the NUS proposing free education and full grants for students. He lost.

After university, Clive embarked on a journalism and military career before becoming an MP. He completed a post-graduate diploma in journalism and worked on local papers before getting onto the BBCs News Trainee Scheme. For more than 10 years he was a BBC TV news reporter, working on several broadcasts in Nottingham, Coventry and Norwich before he became the BBC eastern region's chief political reporter. After that, he worked behind the camera as a BBC technician.

Alongside his journalism, Clive joined the Territorial Army. In 2006 he completed his Royal Military Academy Sandhurst training as an infantry officer with 7 RIFLES (Reserve Infantry Battalion of London South). He experienced a period of depression after a three-month tour of duty in Afghanistan (2009) but was able to recover with counselling. Politicians, like anyone else, may need support to work through difficult experiences.

Clive stood for election in Norwich South and won the seat in May 2015. He is a proud supporter of Norwich City Football Club (Lewis, 2020).

He promised to stand up for the most vulnerable against an "onslaught of cuts" by the governing party. He is passionate about "a fully funded public, not private NHS; for decent, secure, properly paid jobs; an economy that works for all of us, not just a few and where the wealthy pay their way". He has campaigned against the privatisation of local NHS services and worked with local campaign groups to encourage "public ownership of the failing privatised rail industry" (Lewis, 2020).

In June the same year, he became chair of the All-Party Parliamentary Humanist Group and a patron of the Anti-Academies Alliance. He was one of 36 Labour MPs to nominate Jeremy Corbyn in Labour's leadership election.

On 14 April 2016 Clive contributed to a debate on diversity at the BBC. He quoted research by the Sutton Trust that showed the impact that a person's school and university have in accessing areas such as law and journalism. He wondered if removing those details from BBC applications would help to increase diversity in recruitment (HC Deb 14 April 2016).

He was cited as someone who could lead the Labour Party in the future but had to step back after he refused to vote for the Brexit bill, in defiance of the Labour Party's order that all Labour MPs vote in favour of leaving the EU. His leadership priorities were as follows (Clive for Leader, 2019):

- real democracy in our country;

- real democracy in our party;

- a green new deal to tackle climate and environmental emergency;

- a modern economic framework that lifts all in our society,

- championing diversity, equality and progressive values.

In the December 2019 elections, he held his seat with a majority of 12,760 from an electorate of 77,845 with a 66% turnout.

During a debate focused on a scheduled deportation flight to Jamaica in February 2020, Clive showed his anger and disappointment with the government's actions. He noted that despite the government saying, "never again" over the first Windrush scandal, these deportation flights seemed to be a form of "state-sanctioned racism" and serve to encourage such racist behaviour in the whole country (HC Deb 10 February 2020).

Clive is a vice-chair of the following groups:

- All-Party Parliamentary Climate Change Group. They organise events in Parliament enabling cross-party discussion and advancing the understanding of policy issues surrounding climate change.

- All-Party Parliamentary Group for the East of England. They create a strong voice to encourage policies which support investment in the economy of the area.

- All-Party Parliamentary Humanist Group, bringing together non-religious MPs and peers to discuss matters of shared interests.

Clive is the vice-chair of the All-Party Parliamentary Group on Limits to Growth, contributing to the international debate on redefining prosperity. He is also a member of All-Party Parliamentary Group for Governance and Inclusive Leadership, seeking to raise the issue of inclusive leadership in all areas of society.

KATE
OSAMOR

KATE OSAMOR

Constituency: Edmonton
Party: Labour and Co-operative
Years in office: 2015 to present
Ethnicity: Black British (Black African)

Kate was born in 1968 and describes herself as a British-born Nigerian. She grew up in Haringey, North London. Her father died when she was a child, and she remembers her mother working several jobs at a time to care for her and her siblings. Her mother was a member of the Labour Party who became a councillor and deputy leader of Haringey Council. She is now a Baroness in the House of Lords, Baroness Osamor.

Kate completed an access course then went on to complete a degree in International Development at the University of East London where she was diagnosed with dyslexia. Following university, she worked for The Big Issue. Kate then worked as a GP Practice Manager and is a trustee of a charity in Enfield which helps women to cope with economic disadvantage. As an active member of the Labour Party, she joined the National Executive of the Labour Party in 2014.

Kate stood for election in 2015 and won the seat. Shortly after becoming an MP, she became Private Parliamentary Secretary to Jeremy Corbyn MP, the then Leader of the Opposition.

Kate has been a member of several committees including the Parliamentary Select Committee on Education. In January 2016 she became Shadow Minister for Women and Equalities. From June 2016 to 2018 she was the Shadow Secretary of State for International Development. In the December 2019 elections, she held her seat with a majority of 16,015 from an electorate of 65,747 with a 61% turnout.

Since March 2020 she has been a member of the International Development Committee with a particular interest in the impact of aid. She has contributed powerfully to many debates to seek a better outcome for refugees, children in domestic abuse situations, those seeking support from the Windrush Compensation Scheme, those trafficked, forced displacement in Africa and knife crime. She is passionate about social justice, poverty reduction, reducing inequality and funding women's groups.

Kate is chair of the following groups:

- All-Party Parliamentary Group on No Recourse to Public Funds, highlighting the plight of destitute migrants and contributing to the development of policy and legislation.

- All-Party Parliamentary Group on Immigration Detention to raise awareness in parliament about the impact of detention in the UK.

- All-Party Parliamentary Group on Eritrea. It seeks to raise awareness of the human rights abuses that are taking place there and make representations to try to improve the situation.

- All-Party Parliamentary Group on Nigeria which seeks to create a better understanding of issues relating to Nigeria and promote democracy in Nigeria.

Kate is vice-chair of the following:

- All-Party Parliamentary Group on Malawi which seeks to support positive relations between both countries and provide a forum to discuss issues affecting politics, culture, society and the economy in Malawi.

- All-Party Parliamentary Group on Sudan and South Sudan, seeking to promote the cause of peace, human rights, justice and development for all the people of Sudan and South Sudan.

- All-Party Parliamentary Group on Knife Crime and Violence Reduction, which seek to gain a better understanding of the issues and make recommendations.

- All-Party Parliamentary Group on Malaria and Neglected Tropical Diseases.

Kate is a member of the Sickle Cell and Thalassaemia All-Party Parliamentary Group, seeking to reduce inequalities and improve standards of care. These positions all demonstrate her ability to speak up for the most vulnerable and to highlight the impact of policies on Black and other minority communities. She would like to see a much fuller representation of Black and other ethnic minority communities in political bodies and more investment in public services.

BIM
AFOLAMI

BIM AFOLAMI

Constituency: Hitchin and Harpenden
Party: Conservative
Years in office: 2017 to present
Ethnicity: Black British (Black African)

Bim was born in 1986 in Crowthorne, Berkshire. His father moved to the UK in his twenties and became a consultant doctor in the NHS. His mother is a pharmacist and his grandfather was an Anglican vicar.

Bim was educated at Eton College and University College, Oxford where he studied Modern History. He played football for the university team and was in the Oxford Union, serving as vice president. He is very grateful to his parents for the sacrifices they made to give him an exceptional start in life and he wants everyone to have "access to a fantastic education and greater opportunities". He is married to Hetti and they have three boys (Afolami, 2020).

Bim is a fan of rugby and football, supporting Northampton Saints Rugby Union Club and Arsenal FC. Bim has been a school governor for many years and supports charities "that focus on helping people return to work" (Afolami, 2020).

After university, Bim became a corporate lawyer and worked in the City of London. As a corporate lawyer, he advised some of the biggest companies in the UK and across the world. He later became a senior executive at HSBC Bank.

In the December 2019 elections, he held his seat with a majority of 6,895 from an electorate of 76,323 with a 77% turnout. He says that he is in politics to "give back to my country. I am passionate about getting the big decisions right for the next generation – helping businesses to thrive, protecting our green belt and caring for the vulnerable" (Afolami, 2020).

One example of this can be seen in his passionate support for The British Library and their ability to borrow money. In March 2020, he shared that this was core to his beliefs about the power of books to level up, and the impact of intellectual property centres in public libraries to improve entrepreneurship. He has also submitted many written questions around justice, education, housing, business and health and social care. Bim sat on three committees – public accounts, regulatory reform and consolidation bills – resigning from these at the end of 2019.

He is keen on protecting his local high street and small businesses in Hitchin, Harpenden and surrounding villages. He opposes the proposed expansion of Luton Airport and would like to see increased funding for local schools. For a few years he has campaigned against the proposal to build an incinerator in his constituency because of the "detrimental environmental impact...odour from the incinerator... extensive noise and traffic disruption" (Afolami, July 2020). He is also passionate about improving the rail service to and from his constituency.

Bim is chair of the following:

- All-Party Parliamentary Group on Credit Unions. Its aim is to provide a forum for discussing the work of credit unions, helping to bring about legislation that enables them to scale up and provide inclusive financial services for more people.

- All-Party Parliamentary Renewable and Sustainable Energy Group, promoting this energy by keeping Parliamentarians updated on technical policy issues in this area.

- All-Party Parliamentary Group on Financial Markets and Services arranging briefings and debates between senior city practitioners, economists, academics and Parliamentarians.

- Bim is a vice-chair of the All-Party Parliamentary Group on Internet, Communications and Technology, understanding the policy issues that affect this area of life for all stakeholders.

- Bim sits on the All-Party Parliamentary Group for Entrepreneurship. They support and promote entrepreneurship by ensuring that Parliament is kept up to date and conditions remain favourable.

KEMI
BADENOCH

KEMI BADENOCH

Constituency: Saffron Walden
Party: Conservative
Years in office: 2017 to present
Ethnicity: Black British (Black African)

Kemi was born in Wimbledon in 1980. Her parents were of Nigerian origin and returned to Nigeria for a while. Her father was a GP and her mother a professor of physiology. She is married to Hamish, a Conservative councillor and banker, and they have three children.

Kemi spent her childhood in Nigeria and the United States, returning to the UK, age 16. Like many teenagers, she had a part-time job at McDonald's whilst doing her A levels. She attended the Phoenix College in Morden, London.

She studied computer systems engineering at the University of Sussex. She has worked as a software engineer at Logica, a systems analyst at Royal Bank of Scotland, an associate director at the private bank Coutts and a director at The Spectator, a conservative magazine. Early in her working life, she combined work and part-time study gaining a Law degree from Birkbeck, University of London in 2009. She shows herself to be clever, hardworking and flexible with the range and depth of what she has achieved.

She joined the Conservative Party at the age of 25 in 2005. She contested the Dulwich and West Norwood constituency in 2010, won by Labour's Tessa Jowell. She stood to represent the Conservatives on the London Assembly in 2015 and came fifth. On the face of it, she lost. However, as two representatives moved on to become MPs a seat became available and she was able to fill it. It says something about being prepared for when an opportunity arises.

In her maiden speech in 2017, she named her personal heroes as former Prime Ministers Margaret Thatcher and Winston Churchill alongside former soldier, lawyer and MP Airey Neave. She also spoke of how she had returned to the UK when she was 16 with her passport and £100 to study for her A levels. She felt that her FE college had low expectations of its Black and minority ethnic students. Having had a childhood in Nigeria, without water and electricity, under a socialist government, she was keen to become a Conservative politician. She was an outsider who beat the favourite candidate by winning over the locals. She is fully committed to free-market thinking, questions the prevalence of institutional racism, and is keen for refugees to take on British values. She sees free trade and enterprise, not aid, as the solution for many African countries.

Kemi's first role in Parliament was sitting on the Justice Select Committee (September 2017). She then became one of several vice-chairs of the Conservative Party (January 2018). From July 2019 to February 2020 she was the Parliamentary Under-Secretary in the Department for Education.

Kemi supported Brexit and this obviously chimed with her constituents as she was voted in again in December 2019 with an increased majority and 44% of the available votes. She held it with a majority of 27,594 from an electorate of 87,017 with a 73% turnout.

Since February 2020 she has been the Exchequer Secretary at HM Treasury and Parliamentary Under-Secretary of State (Minister for Equalities) in the Government Equalities Office.

More recently several MPs, from all backgrounds, have been questioning the government about the overrepresentation of Black and minority ethnic people in the COVID-19 figures. As the Minister for Equalities Kemi is one of the people tasked with responding to these concerns. She has been answering questions about the government's handling of the pandemic and the disproportionate number of deaths from the Black and minority ethnic communities. She's made several other spoken contributions around gender, basic income, special education needs, school funding, climate change and manufacturing.

On her website she identifies her priorities for her constituency as keeping the community safe, continuing to support the NHS and increasing funding for schools (Badenoch, 2020).

MARSHA DE CORDOVA

MARSHA DE CORDOVA

Constituency: Battersea
Party: Labour
Years in office: 2017 to present
Ethnicity: Black British (Black Caribbean)

Marsha was born in Bristol, England in 1976. She is registered blind having been born with nystagmus. She has five siblings, one of whom is the professional footballer Bobby Decordova-Reid. She studied Law and European Policy Studies at London South Bank University. Following university, she worked for many charities including Action for Blind People. In 2014 she founded the charity London Vision. The charity helps people living with sight loss to access education, and employment and to use technology to live a full life. The charity works with the Thomas Pocklington Trust where Marsha was an engagement and advocacy director prior to becoming an MP.

Marsha gained experience on the work and pensions committee and then became Shadow Minister (work and pensions) for Disabled People. She held this post from October 2017 until April 2020. Currently, she is the Shadow Secretary of State for Women and Equalities.

Marsha was successful in the 2019 elections, winning her seat with a majority of 5,668 from an electorate of 79,350 with a 76% turnout.

During her short time as an MP, Marsha has asked many questions of the government on school exclusions, adults experiencing domestic abuse, social care, transport and jobs. She was able to introduce an important debate on media diversity after she was misidentified in the press by reputable organisations: the BBC, *Evening Standard* and Getty Images. This and many other blunders have been linked to a lack of diversity in journalism and broadcasting, especially at senior levels. Marsha was keen to emphasise that diversity should include race, gender, class and disability. In an interview with Wandsworth Times she stated:

"We have more women of colour in Parliament than ever before and this is something to celebrate. This is sadly undermined though if media can't be bothered to tell us apart" (Krause, 2020).

She has also expressed concerns for the continued funding of law centres, providing access to justice for those who cannot afford to pay for it. She has used opportunities to express anger, upset and worry around the increase in violent crime linked to reduced funding of police, education and youth services.

Many of Marsha's more recent written questions have been concerned with the impact of COVID-19 on child maintenance services, on deaf and disabled people's access to social care, on pregnant women unable to work from home and on blind people's access to essential groceries.

Following the Grenfell Tower fire, Marsha brought to the attention of the House that some of her constituents were living in apartment blocks wrapped in unsafe flammable cladding and wondered about deadlines for making them safe.

In February 2020 Marsha added her voice to that of other MPs asking the government to halt deportation flights back to Jamaica. One of her constituents, who arrived in the UK as a 5-year-old, was being deported after serving a seven-month custodial sentence in 2015.

Marsha has also spoken out against the large number of school exclusions and its correlation to child poverty. There is also the fact that exclusions disproportionally affect Black boys of Caribbean heritage who are 40 times more likely to be excluded than other pupils. She is particularly saddened by the number of pupils with Special Educational Needs (SEND) who are excluded – 418,000 in the academic year 2017–2018. She blames this on budget cuts meaning that schools are unable to provide support. This is based on figures from the National Education Union which estimates a £1bn funding shortfall for SEND provision in mainstream schools (National Education Union, 2020).

Marsha is the Shadow Secretary of State for Women and Equalities. Marsha is chair of the All-Party Parliamentary Group on Eye Health and Visual Impairment which seeks to promote the interests and concerns of blind and partially sighted people.

Marsha is vice-chair of the following:

- All-Party Parliamentary Group for Disability. They work across Parliament for the interests of all disabled people, their families, carers and friends.

- Christians in Parliament All-Party Parliamentary Group. This is an internal group to support Christians of all denominations and parties to work in the Houses of Parliament.

- All-Party Parliamentary Group on Football; they arrange meetings for Parliamentarians and the football authorities to discuss important matters.

- All-Party Parliamentary Human Rights Group, raising the profile of international human rights and investigating when abuses occur.

Marsha is a member of the following groups:

- All-Party Parliamentary Group on Adult Social Care. It's a group where MPs and Lords from all parties try to influence the government policy on social care reform.

- All-Party Parliamentary Group for Council Housing. They seek to increase the number of council houses being built and to represent the interests of council tenants in Parliament.

- All-Party Parliamentary Group for Special Educational Needs and Disabilities, supporting SEND provision in special schools and in mainstream education.

JANET
DABY

JANET DABY

Constituency: Lewisham East
Party: Labour
Years in office: 2018 to present
Ethnicity: Black British (Black Caribbean)

Janet Daby was born in 1970 to a Guyanese Indian father and Black Jamaican mother. Her mum was a nurse in the NHS. She was brought up on a council estate in Lewisham. She experienced physical racism as a child when her windows were pelted with eggs on three consecutive nights. She lived in Deptford and attended Blackheath Bluecoat School in Greenwich. Her parents were part of the Windrush generation that moved to Britain in the 1950s and 1960s. Daby has two children.

Her career has centred on fostering, caring and social care management. She is the Founding Director of The Whitefoot and Downham Community Food Plus Project. Whether working in social care or to reduce food poverty and isolation, Janet's route into politics came from her passion to make positive changes in the area where she lived.

She became a Lewisham borough councillor in 2010, later becoming its Deputy Mayor. She battled against the closure of Lewisham A&E and initiated a Violence Against Women and Girls Strategy. Her other achievements during this time include improved support for families affected by knife crime, increasing awareness of female genital mutilation, saving a local bus route, saving her daughter's nursery from closing and mentoring Black and minority ethnic people who want to get involved in politics (Daby, 2020).

When the sitting MP Heidi Alexander resigned after the Brexit results in 2018, Janet was selected to stand for the seat. She retained the seat for Labour at the June elections with 50.2% of the vote. Lewisham voted 70% to remain. Her majority after the December 2019 elections was 17,008 from an electorate of 67,857 with a 66% turnout.

In Parliament, she has sat on the Justice Committee and the Home Affairs Committee. Currently, she is the Shadow Minister for Housing Communities and Local Government.

More recently Janet has raised questions about health inequalities and the impact of a decade of austerity. In her response to the March 2020 budget, she was able to raise the underfunding of the NHS and the underappreciation of carers who deserve a real living wage, minimum hours and more than their allocated 15 minutes to carry out their care visits. Since COVID-19 more people are aware of the various risks and rewards carers face in their role.

She would like to see more monitoring and focus to reduce health inequalities. Like others before her, she has also called on the General Medical Council, the Nursing & Midwifery Council and the General Pharmaceutical Council to include diversity training on their programmes.

She has submitted written questions on housing for survivors of domestic abuse, bereavement support for unmarried partners, period poverty, food safety, mental health in the workplace and universal credit. She has also raised concerns on privately run prisons, leasehold reform, sale of arms to Saudi Arabi, the impact of leaving the EU without a deal, policing and stop and search. She's also been keeping the government to account on one of her constituents who is British Iranian and being detained in Iran.

She's asked questions about the Grenfell Tower Inquiry, the climate emergency, racism in football, Domestic Abuse Bill, European Union (Withdrawal Agreement) Bill, security funding for places of worship, mental health, immigration, prisons, extremism, NHS, access to criminal justice, the Windrush Compensation Scheme, education, social care, knife crime, refugees and rail travel. This shows the wide range of issues MPs need to keep abreast of, as these affect some of their constituents.

Janet has been one of several MPs challenging the government's attempts to change the legislation around children in care, especially during COVID-19. "As a former social worker and fostering manager, I am deeply concerned about the impact of this legislation." She goes on to show the dangers of removing safeguards and diluting protections at a time when young people are more anxious, stressed and lonely during the coronavirus pandemic (HC 10 June 2020).

In her own constituency, Lewisham East, the National Youth Advocacy Service has three times the number of safeguarding referrals during the lockdown compared to the same period in the previous year. She quotes the Children's Commissioner for England, Anne Longfield who said, "This crisis must not remove protections from extremely vulnerable children, particularly as they are even more vulnerable at this time" (Simpson, 2020).

Janet is the Shadow Minister in the Equalities Office for Faiths, Women and Equalities. She is a vice-chair of the All-Party Parliamentary Group on Dyslexia and other Specific Learning Difficulties. Their aim is to enable individuals with dyslexia to achieve their potential across all sectors and all ages.

She is also a vice-chair of the Sickle Cell and Thalassaemia All-Party Parliamentary Group, seeking to reduce inequalities and improve standards of care.

Janet is a member of the All-Party Parliamentary Group on Parkrun, seeking to support Parkrun and improve public health.

FLORENCE ESHALOMI

FLORENCE ESHALOMI

Constituency: Vauxhall
Party: Labour and Co-operative
Years in office: December 2019 to present
Ethnicity: Black British (Black African)

Florence was born in 1980 in Brixton, London. Florence is of Nigerian descent and the eldest of three girls. Her mum was a teacher and single parent who suffered from sickle cell anaemia and related kidney failure, so Florence became her carer for a while. Florence attended primary schools in Lambeth and completed her A levels at St. Francis Xavier Sixth Form College in Clapham South. Florence is married to Matthew and they have two children, Mia and Malachi. She is active in her local church in Brixton.

Alongside her studies, Florence began working in Sainsbury's super-market from the age of 16. She is the first member of her family to go to university. She obtained a BA Hons in Political and International Studies with Law from Middlesex University. Through the EU funded Erasmus Student Exchange programme, she was able to study in the Netherlands at Utrecht University.

Her civic roles include working in local government as a policy officer and as a regional organiser for the Labour Party. She represented Brixton Hill on Lambeth Borough Council. She has also been a Public Affairs Manager for the Runnymede Trust; the UK's leading race equality think tank.

In 2016 Florence was elected to the London Assembly, repre-senting the Lambeth & Southwark constituencies. On the London Assembly, she became Labour's lead spokesperson on transport issues. As a member of the police and crime committee, she spoke up for girls who may be part of gangs. In an article in May 2019, she warned that if women and girls remain invisible, as perpetrators and victims, then they miss out on the "meaningful protection and support" (Eshalomi, 2019) that are offered to men. She noted that as well as diversion programmes needing a broader appeal, women and mothers were often the ones offering friendship, support and comfort to those who had experienced gang-related violence.

In October 2019 she was selected as the Labour candidate for the Vauxhall constituency, to replace Kate Hoey. She was not the inside candidate but came across as a real person not only a politician.

As columnist Zoe Williams remarks with humour in an article for *The Guardian*, "[Florence] shone as a human being [and] gave the real impression of having met some and thought about their predicament" (Williams, 2019). Florence was elected in December 2019, winning the seat with a majority of 19,612 votes from an electorate of 88,659 with a 64% turnout.

In her maiden speech in January 2020 she shows her pride in representing a vibrant community with people from all over the world and an active LGBTQ community. Fifty languages are spoken in her old primary school in her constituency. The area is home to many cultural venues too such as the Young Vic, the London Eye, MI6, the Southbank Centre and the Kia Oval cricket ground. She pays tribute to her mum whom she describes as a fighter, battling with sickle cell and regular dialysis. Florence celebrates the work of the NHS but also calls for increased funding as it deals with even more demands from people who are experiencing mental health challenges, those who are homeless with complex needs, as well as a rise in children turning up at Accident and Emergency.

She got into politics to "give a voice to people who feel politics isn't for them" (HC Deb 16 January 2020). She spoke of how sad she was by the stabbing of a 15-year-old near her constituency where she was one of the first on the scene and had to call the emergency services. She pleads to us all not to become desensitised to knife crime but to understand the root causes around childhood trauma. She will continue to speak up for "investment in youth services and creating positive experiences for our young people". She will continue to "challenge the Home Office to invest in our police service, so that it has the resources to catch the people who continue to exploit our vulnerable young people". She pledges "to continue to champion and speak up for the young women and young girls facing sexual exploitation" (HC Deb 16 January 2020). All this to the best of her ability.

Florence sits on the committee on the future relationship with the European Union and also in the Opposition Whips office in the House of Commons. She was made aware of an increase in hate crime in her constituency as a result of the terrorist attack in nearby Streatham and wanted assurance from the House that future legislation will protect all citizens.

In a debate on school exclusions, Florence reminded the House of a prison inspectorate report which confirmed that 9 out of 10 people in police custody had been permanently excluded from school. Because of the link between school exclusions and criminal activity, she hopes the government will follow the lead of the Mayor of London and roll out extra school provision across the country.

In a debate around leaseholders and cladding, she reminded the government of the struggle of many leaseholders in buildings with flammable cladding. They cannot sell or re-mortgage their homes and the freeholders have not replaced the flammable cladding despite the Grenfell Tower findings some three years ago (2017). She conveyed that many of her constituents felt trapped in their homes and struggled to sleep at night. She suggested that the government could give technical support to building owners so they could access the funds available and upgrade their buildings, or, give local authorities the power to take over the blocks and carry out the required improvements (HC Deb 5 February 2020).

In response to the March 2020 budget, Florence used the opportunity to raise the concerns of her many self-employed constituents. She wanted the Chancellor to ensure that universal credit was fit for purpose and could payout from day 1 so that constituents avoided unnecessary hardship. Similarly, she wanted the government to consider the position of those who were in rental accommodation and unable to work, either through coronavirus or the closure of certain business sectors. How can central or local government offer temporary support?

In March 2020, Florence raised the concern for persecuted Christians in Nigeria as the UK is meant to be a leader in the championing of freedom of religion or belief. This would be a concern for many of her constituents and she wondered if the UK government could exert any pressure on the Nigerian government.

With the coronavirus affecting all aspects of life, Florence has sought clarification in the House on transport and housing as regards to safety, legislation, availability and funding. She also enquired about emergency childcare provision for young people living with adults who become infected and are hospitalised for COVID-19 (HC 17 March 2020).

Florence is a member of the Sickle Cell and Thalassaemia All-Party Parliamentary Group, seeking to reduce inequalities and improve standards of care. Florence is one of several vice-chairs of the All-Party Parliamentary Group on Nigeria which seeks to promote links between the UK and Nigeria. Florence sits on the All-Party Parliamentary Group on Erasmus, protecting the cohesive exchange of staff, students and apprentices across borders. Florence is a vice-chair of the All-Party Parliamentary Group on Eye Health and Visual Impairment. The group promotes the interests of blind and partially sighted people.

Florence is a vice-chair of the All-Party Parliamentary Group for London, promoting its people, places and businesses.

DARREN
HENRY

DARREN HENRY

Constituency: Broxtowe
Party: Conservative
Years in office: December 2019 to present
Ethnicity: Black British (Black Caribbean)

Darren was born in 1968 and is originally from Bedford. He has been married to Caroline for 21 years. They have young adult twins, one of whom has autism. They also have a cairn terrier called Poppy.

Darren spent 26 years (1987–2013) as a logistics officer and former squadron leader in the Royal Air Force. He was also a rugby union referee. He then retired from the RAF to study logistics management at Lincoln University. He followed this with working for Carillion (2014) as a programme manager, providing facilities for NHS Great Western Hospital. Until November 2015 he worked as the General Manager of Harvest Fine Foods Limited.

Darren joined the Conservative Party in 2014, whilst still in the military. He sought nomination for two Conservative seats but lost the first, North West Hampshire, to the former Deputy Mayor of London, Kit Malthouse, and the second, Wolverhampton North East, to Labour's Emma Reynolds in 2015. Like many MPs, this shows a level of determination and commitment.

From 2017–2019, he was a Conservative councillor for the Till and Wylye Valley division of Wiltshire Council. In early 2019 he was shortlisted to be Police and Crime Commissioner for Swindon and Wiltshire.

When the Conservative Member of Parliament Anna Soubry moved from the Conservative Party, during the debates around the European Union Withdrawal Agreement, the party began to look for a new candidate. Darren beat several others to be chosen as the representative for Broxtowe. In an interview for Nottinghamshire Live in September 2019 he said, "with my long military background, I hold the values of loyalty and integrity" (Locker, 2019).

During his election campaign, Darren suggested that the increasing number of foodbanks was as a result of poor people not being able to budget well. He was called "utterly clueless" (Bartlett, 2019) and lacking in compassion from outraged audience members. Many blame the Conservative austerity and other policies for the increase in food bank use. According to the Trussell Trust, more than 820,000 emergency food parcels were given out between April and September 2019,

26% higher than the same period in 2018. They have 1,200 food bank centres in their network, believed to be two-thirds of all food banks in the UK (Trussell Trust, 2020).

Darren won his seat with a majority of 5,331 from an electorate of 73,052 with a 76% turnout. In his maiden speech, June 2020, he paid tribute to his hardworking parents from the Windrush generation and was clear that he didn't think immigrants could not be Conservatives. "We were a traditional British working-class family: hardworking, loyal, fiercely patriotic – and Conservative". He is "proud to be the first Conservative MP of West Indian heritage – Black, British with all my heart, proud of my West Indian heritage and Conservative to my fingertips" (HC Deb 25 June 2020).

He expresses a passion to support the NHS and lobby the government to expand what is offered at his local Nottingham University Hospital NHS Trust. He claimed that this would include a new Women's and Children's Unit benefitting the families in his constituency of Broxtowe. He pledges to "fight to secure the needs of vulnerable people" (HC Deb 25 June 2020) in his constituency, including those affected by the reform of the Mental Health Act.

Darren is a vice-chair of the All-Party Parliamentary Group on Premature and Sick Babies. It aims to raise awareness of the issues affecting the parents of these babies and to create action which helps to secure the best quality of life for affected families.

KIM
JOHNSON

KIM JOHNSON

Constituency: Liverpool Riverside
Party: Labour
Years in office: December 2019 to present
Ethnicity: Black British

Kim was born in 1960. She is the first Black MP in Liverpool.

She has worked on childcare strategy and Sure Start at the Department of Education and Skills. From 2005–2008, Kim served as the creative diversity manager in Liverpool's Capital of Culture bid team. She is chair of Squash, a café, health and arts initiative that won the BBC Food and Farming Awards Best shop award in 2019.

In her political life, she has been a Unison shop steward for many years and the deputy chair of Unison's National Black Members Committee. She was selected by a panel of national, local and regional party representatives to stand for the Liverpool seat. She became an MP following the December 2019 election. She won the seat with a majority of 37,043 from an electorate of 80,310 with a 66% turnout.

Although active in her community, her journey to Westminister had not been planned. She was selected in a short process to replace long-standing MP Louise Ellman who had made a sudden exit from the Labour Party and politics. In an article in LabourList in November 2019, Kim is described by Labour MP Angela Rayner as a "staunch trade unionist" and a "well-known anti-racist campaigner" (Rodgers, 2019).

Kim is a member of the advisory committee on works of art, the education committee and the women and equalities committee.

During this time of COVID-19, Kim has been challenging the government on employment allowances, the rise in hate crimes and debt relief for developing countries struggling to cope with the pandemic.

In June 2020 she recorded her concerns over the rise in the number of looked-after children and the government's actions to reduce legal protections. She notes that there were "78,000 children in care nationally last year (2019), a 4% rise on the previous year and a shocking 30% rise since 2010". In her own constituency of Liverpool Riverside, "There are nearly 1,500 vulnerable children in care who need these protections, including 115 unaccompanied child asylum seekers" (HC Deb 10 June 2020).

She states that looked-after children are more likely to suffer mental health issues, end up in prison, succumb to addictions and be unemployed, and are less likely to achieve educationally. Given this, she asks "Will loosening the monitoring and support redress the situation?"

Added to this is the steady cut in local authority – "Liverpool City Council has seen its government income slashed by 64% over the past 10 years" (HC Deb 10 June 2020).

Kim is one of several vice-chairs of the All-Party Parliamentary Group on Palestine which seeks to foster good relations between both countries and promote a just and lasting peace in the Middle East.

She is also a vice-chair of the following:

- the All-Party Parliamentary Group on Western Sahara which seeks to promote mutual concern between both countries.

- the All-Party Parliamentary Group on Zimbabwe as it seeks to support democracy in Zimbabwe and foster good relations.

- the All-Party Parliamentary Group on Credit Unions whose aim is to help them grow and be able to offer inclusive financial services for many more people.

- the All-Party Parliamentary Group for Fairtrade. It seeks to raise awareness of the importance of Fairtrade and deepen the relationship between Fairtrade organisations and Parliamentarians.

- the All-Party Parliamentary Group on Freeports, promoting how they can benefit the local and national economy.

Kim sits on the All-Party Parliamentary Group on Domestic Violence and Abuse. They work towards the elimination of domestic violence and abuse, highlight the need for specialist support and develop helpful laws and policies.

Kim is a member of the All-Party Parliamentary Group on International Conservation. This looks at wildlife conservation and biodiversity issues affecting the planet. Kim is a member of the All-Party Parliamentary Group on State Pension Inequality for Women.

ABENA
OPPONG-
ASARE

ABENA OPPONG-ASARE

Constituency: Erith and Thamesmead
Party: Labour
Years in office: December 2019 to present
Ethnicity: Black British (Black African)

Abena was born in London. She studied Politics with International Relations at the University of Kent, following this with a Master's degree in International Law with International Relations.

Abena was a councillor for Erith ward on Bexley Council (2014–2018) where she served as deputy leader of the opposition and shadow cabinet member for Education. She was also a researcher at City Hall, London.

Abena was the first Black woman to be elected onto the Fabian Women's Network Executive Committee (Fabian Women, 2020). She is the first Black chair of the Labour Women's Network, mentoring and training women like her who may have extra barriers in getting into politics. The Labour Women's Network champions all-women shortlists, tackling sexual harassment and abusive language in politics and introducing parental leave arrangements for councillors and MPs. She is also a member of the trade union Unison. She sat on Labour's Race Equality Advisory Group seeking to provide race equality policy ideas. In sticking to her declared goals to increase political participation she has co-authored 'Stand Up and Be Counted: Be a Councillor' providing practical advice for women from a range of backgrounds to stand as councillors.

Abena had several roles in the House of Commons before becoming an MP. She served as a Parliamentary assistant and constituency liaison officer. She also advised the then Shadow Minister for Preventing Violence Against Women and Girls.

Abena won the selection as the Parliamentary candidate for her area against the Greenwich Council cabinet member and GMB union representative Nadine Houghton. Houghton had also been backed by the leadership with endorsements from many of the unions. Undeterred, Abena won the nomination. She held the seat for Labour in December 2019 with a majority of 3,758 from an electorate of 65,399 and a 63% turnout. Abena and Bell are the first MPs of Ghanaian heritage.

In her maiden speech, Abena paid tribute to those trailblazers who had gone before her and those who mentored her. She remembered her Careers Adviser laughing at her when she said she wanted to work in Parliament.

She celebrated the fact that, 100 years after women got the vote, the Parliamentary Labour Party now reflects the gender breakdown in the country, 51% female. She seeks to put Thamesmead on the London transport map. This means getting the Docklands Light Railway (DLR) to include Thamesmead.

She spoke to the stories behind the homelessness crisis such as children living far away from their schools or families living in hostels without a kitchen. Her repeated phrase was "When I see injustice, I always turn anger into action" (HC Deb 29 January, 2020).

On the debate to try to stop the deportation flight to Jamaica in February 2020, Abena shared the story of one of her constituents. He had moved to the UK at the age of five, committed a crime at the age of 17 and served his time. This was many years ago. She asks if it is fair to punish people (by deportation) for mistakes they have already paid for.

In January 2020 she became the Parliamentary Private Secretary to the new Shadow Secretary of State for Environment, Food and Rural Affairs, Luke Pollard. In April of the same year, she became the Parliamentary Private Secretary to the newly appointed Shadow Chancellor of the Exchequer, Anneliese Dodds.

Abena is the Secretary of the All-Party Parliamentary Dance Group. They aim to promote dance as an art form with education and social benefits, and as an important ally in healthy living and the fight against obesity.

Abena is a vice-chair of the All-Party Parliamentary Group for Hockey to support an increase in participation in the sport. Abena is a member of the All-Party Parliamentary Group on Women in Parliament seeking to support women in Parliament and increase the number of them.

Abena has spoken in support of the Fire Safety Bill around the safety of people in tower blocks since the devastating Grenfell fire in June 2017. This is to legislate the responsibility of upgrading safety on the building owners and local authorities, not the tenants. Back in 2017, as the equalities policy led at City Hall (London), Abena was seconded to be a Grenfell community liaison manager.

She has represented her local Sikh Temple by calling for a Sikh ethnic tick box to be on the 2021 Census. She has since found out that this box will not be included.

More recently she has been lobbying the government for support for carers during the COVID-19 crisis. This is mainly supporting a Labour Party call for a "Care for Carers" package offering mental health support for three million NHS carers and staff. The hope is for a 24 hours professionally staffed national hotline to support and treat NHS carers and staff with post-traumatic stress disorder.

She also showed concern for the events industry through the COVID-19 pandemic. She writes that the events sector is worth £42.3 billion to the UK economy with over 25,000 businesses supporting 570,000 jobs. Since the vast majority of summer festivals have been cancelled the impact will be hugely devastating for those employed in the sector.

Abena calls for justice for the family of Belly Mujinga, a transport worker who was spat on by a commuter claiming he had the coronavirus. The commuter also spat on her co-worker. The case has been closed with no consequences. She shared that in June 2020 a man who spat on a police officer in Glasgow was jailed for 12 months.

On 15th June she wrote to the government to request that they continue to fund free school meals throughout the summer as many families, including 3,759 children in her constituency, would be at risk of going hungry without the provision. On the same day many others, including Manchester United footballer Marcus Rashford, lobbied the government for this. Rashford, who had collaborated with food waste charity FareShare to raise £20 million for food for children, was credited with the government's U-turn the following day.

TAIWO
OWATEMI

TAIWO OWATEMI

Constituency: Coventry North West
Party: Labour
Years in office: December 2019 to present
Ethnicity: Black British (Black African)

Taiwo is from Plumstead, London with extended family connections in Coventry. She was six years old when her father died as a result of not finding an organ donor. Her mother, a nurse, raised Taiwo with her twin and elder brother.

Before attending university she undertook an internship with Oliver Letwin, run by Social Mobility Foundation. This gave her experience of the Houses of Parliament and the ins and outs of drafting policy.

She has had a long interest in politics. This was sealed with an incident in her local area whilst she was at university. She remembers her mother telling her that she could either "sit down and do nothing; or go out and make a difference" (Burns, 2020). She chose the latter.

She has a Masters degree in Pharmacy from the University of Kent. She was a member of The Young Fabians, the section of the Fabian Society for those under 31 years of age. The society is a voluntary body, "affiliated to, but distinct from, the Labour party" (The Young Fabians, 2020). Taiwo was vice-chair of the Young Fabian Health Network.

As a senior oncology pharmacist, she specialised in cancer and palliative care. As a pharmacist, she saw the difficulties with accessing medicines for her patients and often wondered if the system was in the best interests of everyone. She also feels her ability to understand policy and its impact on real people in the real world is an asset to her work. She sees it as Labour's duty to be a strong opposition to government policies they disagree with but also to be open to working with different political parties where this is good for constituents.

In the December 2019 elections, she won the Coventry North West seat with a majority of 208 from an electorate of 75,247 and a 63% turnout. It was a close run race with the Conservative candidate.

Her Parliamentary aims are to protect the NHS, end the housing crisis and tackle knife crime.

In April 2020 Taiwo was offered the role of Parliamentary Private Secretary (PPS) to the new Shadow Home Secretary Nick Thomas-Symonds MP. Taiwo sees this as an opportunity to hold the government to account on domestic security and police numbers, whilst hoping to highlight the importance of neighbourhood police officers and the vital role they play in keeping Coventry safe.

Like many MPs Taiwo has been concerned about the impact COVID-19 is having on her constituents. In June 2020 she raised the issue of Rolls-Royce shedding 65 jobs and the impact that would have on the UK since they are the only company welding the veins of plane propellers. She also wanted a support package for theatre and exhibition centres in Coventry as they seem unable to access the government support provided (HC Deb 25 June 2020).

She is chair of the All-Party Parliamentary Group on Alternative Investment Management, raising awareness of the sector and its contribution to the UK economy.

She is also chair of the All-Party Parliamentary Group on Erasmus. They champion the opportunity for staff, students and apprentices to work abroad whilst ensuring the UK remains an attractive place for international students.

Taiwo is a vice-chair of the All-Party Parliamentary Group for the West Midlands, seeking to maximise future investment in the region for the benefit of all its local communities. She is a vice-chair on the Nigeria All-Party Parliamentary Group which seeks to support development and democracy in Nigeria.

BELL RIBEIRO-ADDY

BELL RIBEIRO-ADDY

Constituency: Streatham
Party: Labour
Years in office: December 2019 to present
Ethnicity: Black British (Black African)

Bell was born in Streatham, London in 1985. She is the daughter of Ghanaian immigrants and grew up on a council estate on Brixton Hill.

Bell went to the independent Streatham and Clapham High School. She followed this with a BSc in Biomedical Science with Ethics & Philosophy of Science from the University of Bradford and an MSc in Medical Law & Ethics at Queen Mary University of London in 2007. She also has a Graduate Diploma in Law from BPP Law School.

Her interest in politics started in student activism: to stop a fellow student from being deported and to oppose a far-right MEP from speaking at a university event. Between 2008–2010 she was the National Black Students' Officer for the National Union of Students (NUS), national coordinator of the Student Assembly Against Racism and the national convenor of the NUS's Anti-Racism/Anti-Fascism campaign. Prior to becoming an MP, Bell worked as Chief of Staff to former Labour front-bencher Diane Abbott MP.

On her website she describes herself as follows: "I am a Black working-class woman, Christian and lifelong socialist who grew up in a Labour family" (Ribeiro-Addy, 2020). This gave the electorate a clear choice between her and the other candidates. Bell was elected in December 2019 with a majority of 17,690. Bell and Abena are jointly the first women of Ghanaian heritage in the UK Parliament.

She sits on the Women and Equalities Committee. She is also a school governor and a member of Labour's Socialist Campaign Group.

In her maiden speech in January 2020, Bell shared that her first foray into politics was campaigning for the previous Streatham MP Chuka Umunna. Having worked with Diane Abbott for years she could see the impact of being an MP but found herself personally affected by the amount of abuse Diane received.

She explores the role of global Britain and how it needs to heal from the wounds of the past before it can truly move forward. These wounds are around slavery, and the apparent impossibility for the government to apologise and pay reparations. She suggests that an easier place to start might be to return stolen treasures, cancel debts already repaid and really apply fair trade rules (HC Deb 30 January 2020).

In a poignant moment, she shared that in the 1700s 50 members of the House (like her) represented slave plantations (who enslaved people who look like her). She has since found out that the UK had taken out a loan of £300bn to pay off slave owners and this was only repaid in 2015. This was paid off by taxpayers, some of whom were the descendants of slaves!

She also makes a plea for the victims of the Grenfell Tower, those who died and those left traumatised and homeless by the experience, the need for better community policing, increased investment in youth services and crime prevention to end the scourge of knife crime.

She refers to the refugee crisis and various climate emergencies to show the need for a more international approach. This is even more so now with the coronavirus. She implores the government to stop treating asylum seekers as second class beings and behaving as if claiming asylum is a crime (HC Deb 4 March 2020).

Very early in her Parliamentary career, Bell was faced with a terrorist attack in her constituency, February 2020. Although she was very grateful to the emergency services for their quick response, she wanted to know that the government had done all it could to prevent the attack from occurring.

In January 2020, Bell was appointed Shadow Minister for Immigration but lost that position when Keir Starmer became the Labour Leader.

In February 2020, the *Evening Standard* used Bell's image in a story about fellow MP Marsha de Cordova. Bell later told BBC News "We are not given the same respect as our white counterparts and that's not right" (BBC News, 4 February 2020). It is even more complicated as the original story was about the BBC Parliament captioning Marsha de Cordova MP as the then Labour Deputy leadership hopeful, Dawn Butler. Bell shared that she was often mistaken for Dawn Butler MP when she was chief of staff to the then Shadow Home Secretary Diane Abbott. All the publications have since apologised but it must be truly irritating that, despite representing diverse communities or being in a senior position, Black woman are not seen in their individuality. Bell suggested that part of the problem was the lack of diversity in most newsrooms, and the tendency of journalists to treat Black, Asian and minority ethnic MPs as part of a homogenous group. As I write there have been several other errors, misidentifying Black male actors, sportspeople and rappers.

In a debate on the Windrush compensation scheme, Bell joined other Labour MPs in challenging the scope of the Bill. Labour would like to change the amount of money offered, the types of compensation awarded, eligibility criteria and the publicity around the scheme. Nevertheless, they supported the scheme as some compensation is better than none. She used the debate as an opportunity to address the victims of the Windrush scandal and their loved ones.

"Some of the people who were treated so terribly died before they ever received any apology, let alone compensation from this Government. People were denied drivers' licences. They were made unemployed. They lost their homes and were put in immigration detention centres. Some were deported, and others were refused re-entry to this country after they had briefly been overseas, breaking up their families. They were British citizens, and this is still happening to them and their loved ones" (HC Deb 10 February 2020). She stated that she will not rest until this injustice is brought to an end.

In March 2020 she was one of several Labour MPs calling for the release of people in detention centres because of their risk of catching COVID-19 in those conditions. She thought they were there because of the government's "arbitrary net migration targets" and they would eventually be freed.

On 22nd June 2020, the second Windrush Day, Bell called on the government to pay the compensation due to victims, only 5% of whom have received any compensation. A few days later and in the wake of the coronavirus, she joined with 21 other Labour MPs calling for a Green New Deal for "climate action to be at the heart of everything our country does as we rebuild" (Ribeiro-Addy, 25 June 2020).

Bell is one of two vice-chairs of the All-Party Parliamentary Group (APPG) on Immigration Detention. The aims are to raise awareness, share research, advocate, connect experts and listen to those who have experience of immigration detention in the UK.

Bell is a member of the All-Party Parliamentary Group on Knife Crime and Violence Reduction, looking at root causes to the problem and seeking preventative measures. She is also a member of the Sickle Cell and Thalassaemia All-Party Parliamentary Group, seeking to reduce inequalities and improve standards of care.

Bell is a member of the "Excluded APPG whose aim is to campaign for financial support for the thousands left behind by the Government's income support schemes" (Ribeiro-Addy, 9 July 2020).

CLAUDIA
WEBBE

CLAUDIA WEBBE

Constituency: Leicester East
Party: Labour
Years in office: December 2019 to present
Ethnicity: Black British (Black Caribbean)

Claudia was born in Leicester in 1965 and grew up in the city. She studied Social Science at De Montfort University in Leicester and followed this with a Masters in Race and Ethnic Relations at Birkbeck, University of London. She is one of the few MPs mentioned here who had a full political life before being elected as a Member of Parliament.

In the 1990s she founded Operation Trident Independent Advisory Group with other community activists. In a Guardian column, Claudia notes that Operation Trident was set up because "90% of homicide victims were black, mainly black men (and) the police response was woeful." She referred to an inquiry by Sir John Hoddinott, former chief constable of Hampshire, who found that the police had a better relationship with the "criminal informants" than it did with law-abiding Black people (Webbe, 2013). Claudia led the media campaigns of the group before becoming its chair.

After the Stephen Lawrence Inquiry (2000) the Met commissioner and Home Secretary agreed to a dedicated Trident operational command unit with 160 officers. They worked alongside the advisory group, who were able to engage with witnesses, victims and members of the community. In 2010 it was threatened with funding cuts, and in February 2012 it was combined with the team who were addressing violent crimes against young people led by then-Mayor of London, Boris Johnson, and called Trident Gang Crime Command. Claudia, the co-founder and former chairwoman, and other members of the advisory group were told that their services were no longer required. The membership and chairing of the group had been taken on by the police, widening the range of locations, organisations, charities, trusts and ethnicities involved. The knowledge around the intricacies of solving Black on Black crime is no longer the focus.

Claudia worked as an adviser to London Mayor Ken Livingstone and was part of his election campaign team. She has worked on anti-racist campaigns including the Anti-Racist Alliance and the National Assembly Against Racism. She has been the director of the Westminister Race Equality Council.

In April 2007 when the then Prime Minister Tony Blair commented that the Black community needed to denounce the gang culture that is killing innocent young Black boys, she wrote a response in *The Guardian* newspaper demonstrating how the real story was different. She named the many community-based resources such as Saturday schools which had been depleted over the years. Also, many grant-giving bodies and inner-city regeneration schemes did not involve the Black community in their decision-making processes (Webbe, 2007).

On the other hand, she identifies that the Black "voluntary, community and faith organisation had historically stepped up to the challenge to provide vital grassroots self-help organisations so as to meet the needs of our vulnerable children and young people and challenge inequality and racism" (Webbe, 2007).

In 2010, Claudia was elected to Islington Council and was re-elected in 2014 and 2018. She served there as a Cabinet Member for Environment and Transport. In 2016 she became a member of Labour's National Executive Committee. In July 2018 she was elected unopposed to be the chair of the disputes panel. She is attuned to societal problems resulting from poverty, unemployment, policing tactics, racism and inequality.

Claudia was nominated to represent the city of her birth, Leicester, and won her seat in December 2019. She got a majority of 6,019 votes from an electorate of 78,433 with a 63% turnout. She is the first female MP for Leicester East.

Claudia sits on many Parliamentary committees including environmental audit, foreign affairs and controls on arms export.

Claudia is a vice-chair on the All-Party Parliamentary Group on Air Pollution which brings together experts and Parliamentarians to find solutions to the problem of poor air quality.

Claudia is a vice-chair on the All-Party Parliamentary Group on the East Midlands, bringing together peers and MPs to work with local government, commerce and civil society to maximise future investment and benefit all its communities.

Claudia is a member of the All-Party Parliamentary Group on Knife Crime and Violence Reduction, evaluating the policies aimed at reducing knife crime and recommending preventative measures, alongside the cross-party Youth Violence Commission.

Claudia is a member of the All-Party Parliamentary Group on Youth Affairs, raising the profile of issues that concern young people whilst encouraging dialogue and a coherent approach to policy.

CONCLUDING THOUGHTS

The Black MPs elected in the December 2019 elections represent the two main political parties of Conservative and Labour. Each of them demonstrates a unique combination of passion and success, ambition and achievements.

Many of the MPs identified in this book are first or second-generation British. Some had parents who came during the Windrush whilst others have ancestral links in the UK and Africa. Many of their parents (or grand-parents) would have grown up in the Commonwealth and had a sense of being British despite living elsewhere.

In whatever way these MPs came to be born and to live in the United Kingdom, they have certainly settled here and want to contribute to civic society. None of us choose where we're born and where our parents come from. They've decided to seek to represent their area and have succeeded in this. Some have moved to different parts of the country and have stood for many elected positions before becoming MPs. They are determined and committed, not easily put off by initial failure.

Despite many of them being the first to do something or represent a group, they are surprisingly normal. There are a few tried and tested ways to become an MP and this is no different for Black MPs.

They have come through some of the main routes that white MPs come through. There is something about the role of a politician that benefits from these backgrounds. There are other routes taken by, "career politicians" that may not yet be an option for a Black person wanting to become an MP. Of the 22 Black MPs included in this book they have come via these well-known routes identified below:

- Public school, Oxbridge and the City

- Legal profession, lawyers and barristers

- Journalism, media and PR

- Trade union activism

- Community and charity work

- Public sector jobs in education and the NHS

- Armed forces

- Local councillor

People become Parliamentary representatives for a range of reasons. Some are called by the knowledge and skills needed for the job. Others are drawn to the tasks involved, the status and associated events. Others find themselves pushed by things they want to change or can't turn a blind eye to. They must eventually convince others of their ability and passion and then campaign for votes. As members of the public, it is in our interest to see the most capable, knowledgeable and whole-hearted people put themselves forward to govern us. We do not help ourselves by dissuading good people from putting themselves forward and leaving a space for those with big egos who only seek power.

These Black politicians, like many of us, will have imperfect lives. They include people from different class, gender, education, ability and dis-ability statuses. They represent a range of lifestyles – single, married, divorced, parents and not parents. Just like us, their lives are a patch-work of different roles, thoughts, feelings and behaviours. Through their passion and path, we see what is possible. This may not be your dream, and it is not mine, but it might encourage you to think big and step into the life that is possible for you. So many skills are learnt with focused effort and practice.

I wrote this book because I realise that many people, including those advising young people and young people themselves, may not be aware of the range of voices and routes into this impactful position. I am pas-sionate about giving people a wide range of role-models, so they know what is possible for them and the different ways to get there. The more you discover successful people who look like you the better equipped you are to make good choices. If someone like you has done it before you already know it is possible.

I hope in these mini-biographies you find someone you can relate to, whether that is because of their ethnicity, their achievements or their passions. If you find your MP in these pages, then reach out to them and ask a few questions to find out more about their day-to-day work. Many welcome constituents to their offices, to show how hard they're working and to publicise their commitment to their role. Do share with friends and family to ensure everyone who could be encouraged by this book will have a chance to read it.

If you or anyone you know would like to become an MP, then I sug-gest you look at the various examples here for inspiration. Think about the impact you would like to have and the difference you can make. Contact your local councillors and MP to find out more about what they do and explore the possibility of shadowing them or volunteering to help. You can also sign up with UK Parliament Week (1–7 November) for resources and updates. You can start anywhere, from school council to neighbourhood watch. You can connect with me @shirleyanstis on Twitter, to share your feedback and help others to find out about this unique book.

Your calling isn't something that somebody can tell you about. It's what you feel. It is the thing that gives you juice. The thing that you are supposed to do. And nobody can tell you what that is. You know it inside yourself.

— Oprah Winfrey

GLOSSARY

I started writing this book after the 2017 general elections. There was an increase in diversity in the House of Commons and I wanted to capture the moment through a book. But it has taken a while to complete and during this time we have lived through the Windrush scandal, the Grenfell Tower fire, Brexit, COVID-19 and the emergence of the Black Lives Matter movement.

Windrush Scandal – The name relates to the Empire Windrush which brought people from the Caribbean from 1948. Caribbean people, from the Commonwealth, were invited to help rebuild Britain after the Second World War. They were British citizens and had the right to settle in the UK granted by the British Nationality Act in 1948. But when the Conservative government introduced their "hostile environment" policies, designed to make it difficult for illegal immigrants to settle, many from the Windrush generation found themselves being caught up by this policy. They had lived and worked here for decades but some of them had not got their British citizenship sorted out and their old documents meant that they were now technically undocumented. They were wrongly detained, denied legal rights, threatened with deportation and some deported by the Home Office. Many who left the Caribbean as children to join working parents, were now parents and grandparents of British people. Many of these cases are still unresolved and the cry for compensation continues. Several MPs raised the awful and shocking situation many people found themselves in and the delays in sorting cases, stopping deportations and paying compensation. Many people lost jobs and homes and became destitute. Many of the MPs in this book spoke up for the many victims affected and put pressure on the government to remedy the effects of a system which most people now think was wrong.

The Grenfell Tower – In June 2017 there was a fire in Grenfell Tower, a 24-storey block of flats in North Kensington, London. It is thought that 72 people died, 70 others were injured and 223 escaped. It's seen as the worst residential fire since the Second World War. The inquiry into the causes for the fire began in September 2017 and is not yet complete. The fire spread rapidly because of the building's cladding and insulation. Some residents were also told to stay in their flats and wait to be rescued but firefighters could not get to them. The building burned for 60 hours before it was eventually extinguished. The inquiry continues to find the reasons and learning from this dreadful incident. Many politicians raise concerns for their constituents who died or were injured, those still in temporary accommodation and those in similar buildings with flammable cladding, that have not yet been made safe.

Brexit (Britain's Exit/the European Union Withdrawal Agreement) – David Cameron gave in to pressure from inside the Conservative Party to hold a referendum on British membership of the European Union in 2016. The referendum results for the UK was that 51.9% voted to leave and 48.1% voted to remain.

There was further discussion on exactly how the UK would leave the European Union. Prime Minister Theresa May took over when David Cameron stepped down, but she was unable to get MPs to agree on a clear way ahead. Boris Johnson based his Conservative leadership campaign on being able to get MPs to agree and eventually to secure a Brexit deal with Europe. He did get MPs to agree, but that was to a no-deal Brexit.

The UK stopped being a member of the European Union (EU) on 31st January 2020. This is followed by an 11-month transition period in which the details of rights, trade agreements and financial responsibilities will be debated, and deals signed. Members of Parliament from all parties were divided in being for or against Brexit. Voters across the country were similarly split.

Black Lives Matter (BLM) – This is many things at once. It is a movement to try to stop the way in which Black people seem to suffer just for being Black. It was started in America (in 2013) by three Black women – Alicia Garza, Patrisse Cullors and Opal Tometi in response to the deaths of young Black men at the hands of law enforcement.

The recent protests are the result of George Floyd being killed by a US police officer who knelt on his neck for more than eight minutes whilst his colleagues filmed it.

Although similar events have been happening for some time, the video evidence, in this case, made everyone sick – those who knew what was happening and those who didn't. What began as solidarity with African Americans extended to looking at similar injustices here in the UK. The statistics on employment, promotion, education, mental health, housing and criminal justice all show a lesser regard for Black lives. More recently with the COVID-19 pandemic, the NHS is also being asked to explain why a disproportionate number of Black lives have been lost, whether staff or patient.

The David Lammy Review of the criminal justice system highlighted the disproportionate negative outcomes for Black people. The Windrush Lessons Learned Review showed the negative impact of the Government's hostile environment on Black people and others from the Commonwealth. Both have been discussed in the House of Commons and neither have been fully implemented.

Several Members of Parliament continue to ask the government to investigate the reasons for the high number of COVID-19 deaths for people from Black, Asian and minority ethnic backgrounds. Many have asked for the NHS and other institutions to be required to risk assess Black and other staff at increased risk before putting them on front line duty. The debate continues as does the pandemic.

On 8 September 2020 MPs discussed the History Curriculum taught in schools, looking at how Black history is included. The debate recognised the African unit guarding Hadrian's Wall in the third century AD, a small Black community in the court of King James IV and the many Black people in England from the 1500s. Black British history began long before the transatlantic slave trade and continues to this day.

MPs continue to ask questions around all the issues mentioned here. They are using their lives to improve their communities and contributing to how we are governed. Politicians, sportspeople, actors, musicians and many non-famous people have been protesting for people to be treated fairly and not be disadvantaged because of their ethnicity or race. Unfortunately, as more people have become aware of the struggle Black people can have just to access a normal life, others have become defensive and even more racist. It remains to be seen if and what gains for equality and inclusion will be made. It takes all of us, using whatever influence we have, to make our communities safe and just. The African American civil rights leader and Nobel Peace Prize winner Martin Luther King Jr once said, "True peace is not merely the absence of tension; it is the presence of justice."

ATTRIBUTIONS & REFERENCES

Official portraits photographs shared are by:

Chris McAndrew (Diane Abbott, Kwasi Kwarteng, Chi Onwurah, Clive Lewis, Kemi Badenoch, Marsha de Cordova)

Richard Townsend (Mark Hendrick, Adam Afriyie, Dawn Butler, James Cleverly, Kate Osamor, Bim Afolami, Janet Daby)

David Woodfall (David Lammy, Helen Grant, Florence Eshalomi, Bell Ribeiro-Addy, Abena Oppong-Asere, Taiwo Owatemi, Claudia Webbe, Darren Henry, Kim Johnson).

Cover illustrations are adapted from the official portrait photographs.

All portraits UK Parliament under Creative Commons Attribution 3.0 Unported (CC BY 3.0) license.

Introduction

HC Deb, (2020). *The Immigration Bill* [Hansard]. vol. 670, 2.15pm. Available at: hansard.parliament.uk/Commons/2020-01-30/debates/33EA2EAC-BA44-490B-93D0-11799618B342/GlobalBritain.

Diane Abbott

HC Deb, (1987). *The Immigration Bill* [Hansard]. vol. 122, 6.49pm. Available at: hansard.parliament.uk/Commons/1987-11-16/debates/3c372344-c6e4-4701-800b-78466232620b/ImmigrationBill#contribution-c3056127-e96a-4dae-aa85-e5bbf6936d7f.

HC Deb, (2016). *Foreign Aid Expenditure* [Hansard]. vol. 611, 7.34pm. Available at: hansard.parliament.uk/Commons/2016-06-13/debates/ED517776-2FB8-4D2E-A959-4CCDC6ACACB5/ForeignAidExpenditure.

HC Deb, (2017). *UK Elections Abuse And Intimidation* [Hansard]. vol. 627, 4.55pm. Available at: hansard.parliament.uk/Commons/2017-07-12/debates/577970DD-1AEF-4071-8AE0-3E3FC6753C6A/UKElectionsAbuseAndIntimidation.

David Lammy

HC Deb, (2018). *Windrush 70Th Anniversary* [Hansard]. vol. 642, 3.11pm. Available at: hansard.parliament.uk/Commons/2018-06-14/debates/0661DB22-68A9-4F6C-9C69-4F42C9837511/Windrush70ThAnniversary.

HC Deb, (2020). *Lammy Review* [Hansard]. vol. 678, 1.33pm. Available at: hansard.parliament.uk/Commons/2020-06-30/debates/9846E64F-6A5D-44E5-A98F-4CB6D65D90AF/LammyReview.

Dawn Butler

HC Deb, (2017). *UN International Day For The Elimination Of Racial Discrimination* [Hansard]. vol. 623, 2.30pm. Available at: hansard.parliament.uk/Commons/2017-03-21/debates/358A8DEF-77B5-4882-8C0B-C3F2C48B39F1/UNInternationalDayForTheEliminationOfRacialDiscrimination.

Kwasi Kwarteng

The Bow Group (2020). Available at: twitter.com/bowgroup.

Chi Onwurah

McDonald, C., (2018). 'Most Influential Women in UK IT 2018: Entrants to the Hall of Fame'. Computer Weekly. Available at: www.computerweekly.com/news/252444993/Most-Influential-Women-in-UK-IT-2018-Entrants-to-the-Hall-of-Fame.

Clive Lewis

Lewis, C., (2020). 'Clive Lewis, MP for Norwich South'. Labour. Available at: www.clivelewis.org/about/.

HC Deb, (2016). *BBC Diversity* [Hansard]. vol. 608, col. 576. Available at: hansard.parliament.uk/Commons/2016-04-14/debates/16041436000002/BBCDiversity.

Clive for Leader, (2019). Five from Clive: my pledges. *Clive for Leader*. Available at: www.cliveforleader.com/what/.

HC Deb, (2020). *Deportation Flight To Jamaica* [Hansard]. vol. 671, col. 589. Available at: hansard.parliament.uk/Commons/2020-02-10/debates/ CA8268EA-7EBF-4DA9-B46D-2EB86F6236BD/DeportationFlightToJamaica.

Bim Afolami

Afolami, B., (2020). About Bim Afolami. *Bim Afolami MP for Hitchin & Harpenden*. Available at: www.bimafolami.co.uk/about-bim-afolami.

Afolami, B., (2020). Stop the Incinerator Campaign. *Bim Afolami MP for Hitchin & Harpenden*. Available at: www.bimafolami.co.uk/news/ stop-incinerator-campaign.

Kemi Badenoch

Badenoch, K., (2020). My priorities for our constituency. *Kemi Badenoch MP for Saffron Walden*. Available at: www.kemibadenoch.org.uk/ my-priorities-our-constituency.

Marsha de Cordova

Krause, R., (2020). Marsha de Cordova speaks out after media mistake her for two other Black MPs. *Wandsworth Times*. Available at: https://www.wandsworthguardian.co.uk/news/18212196. marsha-de-cordova-speaks-media-mistake-two-black-mps/.

National Education Union, (2020). SEND Crisis. *National Educational Union*. Available at: neu.org.uk/funding/send-crisis.

Janet Daby

Daby, J., (2020). About Janet. *Labour*. Available at: www.janetdaby.org/ about/.

HC Deb, (2020). *Children And Young Persons* [Hansard]. vol. 677, col. 347. Available at: hansard.parliament.uk/Commons/2020-06-10/ debates/5964F78B-8FEA-441B-A146-889607FBFA21/ ChildrenAndYoungPersons.

Simpson, F., (2020).'Children & Young People Now.' MIA Education. Available at: www.cypnow.co.uk/news/article/

children-s-commissioner-for-england-government-must-revoke-changes-to-statutory-duties.

Florence Eshalomi

Eshalomi, F., (2019). 'We must not forget the girls involved with London's gangs'. On London. Available at: www.onlondon.co.uk/florence-eshalomi-we-must-not-forget-the-girls-involved-with-londons-gangs/.

Williams, Z., (2019). How to replace Kate Hoey? My local party showed that stitch-ups aren't working. *The Guardian*. Available at: www.theguardian.com/commentisfree/2019/oct/28/replace-kate-hoey-local-party-stitch-ups-not-working.

HC Deb, (2020). *Health And Social Care* [Hansard]. vol. 669 col. 1227. Available at: hansard.parliament.uk/Commons/2020-01-16/debates/8FF34846-E79D-40FD-9B8C-B0DF1CDC96F6/HealthAndSocialCare.

HC Deb, (2020). *Local Government Finance* [Hansard]. vol. 671, col. 360. Available at: hansard.parliament.uk/Commons/2020-02-05/debates/2EAB80D8-C522-4441-9390-250FA9E16ACF/LocalGovernmentFinance.

HC Deb, (2020). 'Question for the Department of Education'. UK Parliament. Available at: questions-statements.parliament.uk/written-questions/detail/2020-03-17/30890.

Darren Henry

Locker, J., (2019). Conservatives select former RAF squadron leader to contest Broxtowe seat. *Nottingham Post*. Available at: www.nottinghampost.com/news/local-news/conservatives-select-former-raf-squadron-3332916.

Bartlett, N., (2019). Tory candidate Darren Henry says people who use food banks 'struggle' to budget. *Daily Mirror*. Available at: www.mirror.co.uk/news/politics/tory-candidate-darren-henry-says-21050908.

HC Deb, (2020). *Covid-19 Support For UK Industries* [Hansard]. vol. 677, col. 1540. Available at: hansard.parliament.uk/

Commons/2020-06-25/debates/E1479A23-8697-4B2E-9E5F-2A208EC3E217/
Covid-19SupportForUKIndustries.

The Trussell Trust (2020). Available at: www.trusselltrust.org.

Kim Johnson

Rogers, S., (2019). 'Kim Johnson chosen to replace Louise Ellman in
Liverpool Riverside'. LabourList. Available at: labourlist.org/2019/11/
kim-johnson-chosen-to-replace-louise-ellman-in-liverpool-riverside/.

HC Deb, (2020). *Children And Young Persons* [Hansard]. vol. 677,
col. 344. Available at: hansard.parliament.uk/Commons/2020-06-10/
debates/5964F78B-8FEA-441B-A146-889607FBFA21/
ChildrenAndYoungPersons.

Abena Oppong-Asare

Fabian Women, (2020). FWN Montering: A Life-Changing Experience.
Fabian Women. Available at: fabianwomen.org.uk/2015/06/07/
fwn-mentoring-a-life-changing-experience/.

HC Deb, (2020). *Homelessness* [Hansard]. vol. 670, col. 865.
Available at: hansard.parliament.uk/Commons/2020-01-29/
debates/8FF4A774-F2B6-4BCA-B5A8-D304E5B33FBB/Homelessness.

Taiwo Owatemi

Burns, C., (2020). 'Taiwo Owatemi: Like every pharmacist in the country,
I've been frustrated by medicines shortages'. The Pharmaceutical Journal.
Available at: www.pharmaceutical-journal.com/news-and-analysis/
opinion/qa/taiwo-owatemi-like-every-pharmacist-in-the-country-ive-
been-frustrated-by-medicines-shortages/20207541.article?firstPass=false.

The Young Fabians, (2020). Who are the Young Fabians? *Nation Builder*.
Available at: www.youngfabians.org.uk/about.

HC Deb, (2020). *Covid-19 Support For UK Industries* [Hansard].
vol. 677, col. 1556. Available at: hansard.parliament.uk/
Commons/2020-06-25/debates/E1479A23-8697-4B2E-9E5F-2A208EC3E217/
Covid-19SupportForUKIndustries

Bell Ribeiro-Addy

Ribeiro-Addy, B., (2020). 'About Bell'. Bell Ribeiro-Addy MP. Available at: bellribeiroaddy.com/about-bell/.

HC Deb, (2020). *Global Britain* [Hansard]. vol. 670, col. 993. Available at: hansard.parliament.uk/Commons/2020-01-30/ debates/33EA2EAC-BA44-490B-93D0-11799618B342/GlobalBritain.

HC Deb, (2020). *Support For Refugees* [Hansard]. vol. 672, col. 327WH. Available at: hansard.parliament.uk/Commons/2020-03-04/ debates/0DA97028-C6CA-4C3A-918D-C76B0A582FFC/ AsylumDecisions(SupportForRefugees).

BBC News, (2020). Caption mix-ups show lack of respect for black MPs. *BBC*. Available at: www.bbc.co.uk/news/uk-politics-51374401.

HC Deb, (2020). *Windrush Compensation Scheme (Expenditure) Bill* [Hansard]. vol. 671, col. 666. Available at: hansard.parliament. uk/Commons/2020-02-10/debates/2689E446-2379-4EFE-8B10- 8E1E0CEC7466/WindrushCompensationScheme(Expenditure)Bill.

Ribeiro-Addy, B., (2020). 'Bell renews call for Green New Deal'. Bell Ribeiro-Addy. Available at: bellribeiroaddy.com/ bell-renews-call-for-green-new-deal/.

Ribeiro-Addy, B., (2020). 'Joining the Excluded APPG'. Bell Ribeiro-Addy. Available at: bellribeiroaddy.com/joining-the-excluded-appg/.

Claudia Webbe

Webbe, C., (2013). Operation Trident is effectively over – now we are all vulnerable. *The Guardian*. Available at: www.theguardian.com/ commentisfree/2013/mar/14/operation-trident-effectively-over-murder.

Webbe, C., (2007). A kick in the teeth from Tony Blair. *The Guardian*. Available at: www.theguardian.com/commentisfree/2007/apr/12/ akickintheteeth.

Printed by Amazon Italia Logistica S.r.l.
Torrazza Piemonte (TO), Italy

41402922R00063